Just T

M000232573

By Patrick Costello

For my father.

*My hero, my mentor, my father, my
partner, and most of all, my friend.
No son has ever had such a cohort
in a jam, on stage, or in life.*

Special thanks go to my Patreon sponsors for helping us
make this book happen.
I love you all.

ISBN: 0-9744190-7-9

Cover art by Carlos Vazquez. Thank you, my brother.

My sincerest heartfelt thanks to
Ken Brewer – he knows why.

Here we stand before your door,
As we stood the year before;
Give us whiskey, give us gin,
Open the door and let us in.
Or give us something nice and hot.
Like a steaming bowl of pepper pot!

~The Philadelphia Mummers

Birdsong brings relief to my longing
I'm just as ecstatic as they are,
but with nothing to say!
Please universal soul, practice
some song or something through me!

~Mewlana Jalaluddin Rumi

Even a fish would stay out of trouble if it
kept its mouth shut!

~My father

Contents

Introduction

The Arkansas Traveler is a very old skit performed by minstrels, medicine show performers, and Vaudevillians. The premise is simple. A gentleman from the city stops in front of a dilapidated shack to ask directions from a farmer.

The city fellow asks questions and gets funny responses from the farmer as he plays his banjo.

> **City Feller**: "Hey, farmer! You been livin' here all your life?"
> **Farmer:** "Not yet."

After each back and forth, the farmer plays a bit of a tune on his banjo.

> **City Feller:** "Hey, farmer! Where does this road go?"
> **Farmer:** "Been livin' here all my life; it ain't gone nowhere yet."

> **City Feller:** "Hey, farmer! Thought you said that mud-hole weren't very deep?"
> **Farmer:** "Only comes up to here on my ducks."

> **City Feller:** "Hey, farmer! You don't know very much, do you?
> **Farmer:** "No, but I ain't lost."

Near the end of the skit, the city feller gets frustrated.

City Feller: "There isn't much between you and a fool!"

Farmer: "Just this banjo."

I love that last joke. It could very well be the story of my life. I have navigated through life with nothing shielding me from the world but my banjo and guitar.

I started playing the banjo to win a bet, but my dream was to be a guitar player. My first guitar was an instrument I salvaged from the trash and patched together with duct tape. I was not sure how to get started, but then I ran across this quote from Woody Guthrie:

> The worst thing that can happen is to cut yourself loose from the people. And the best thing is to sort of vaccinate yourself right into the big streams and blood of the people.

I took my banjo and my crappy guitar to the city — no idea of where to go, no money in my pockets and no goal in mind. Into the streets, out into the night and the bloodstream of the city. Nothing between me and the world but my instruments.

I met saints and sinners. I made music with and for Mafiosos and the IRA. I have sung for and with the sick, lonely, and crazy. I played for millionaires and jammed with a man so poor he did not own matching shoes.

I had no armor or protection. Just this banjo.

That is what this book is about. Simple as that.

The Rabbit

It was show-and-tell time at Raggedy Anne and Andy Nursery School in Wheaton, Illinois. For reasons I can no longer remember, I had nothing to share with the group.

I can remember a palatable sense of fear as each of my classmates stood up to share some treasure from home. I was furiously praying for my mom to wander in with my show and tell item – and if that did not happen, maybe the teacher would skip me. Yes! Perhaps I would not get called!

"Joseph?" Our teacher snapped me out of my reverie. "Do you have something to share?"

Without hesitating or stopping to think about what to do next, I went into a pitch about my amazing invisible rabbit. I talked about how ordinary pets couldn't go to school, but you can take an invisible rabbit anywhere! I went through the motions of picking up an invisible cage, opening its invisible door, reaching in and gently picking up my invisible rabbit.

I held out my invisible rabbit for the kids to see. They were all impressed — Oohs and ahhs from around the room.

Since things were going well, I handed the invisible rabbit to one of the kids and allowed everybody to stroke its invisible fur before passing it along. Everybody was very gentle. Once the rabbit got back to me, I tossed it back in its cage, and that was the end of that – or so I thought.

The next day one of the kids remembered my rabbit. Upon request, I produced the invisible cage, and pretty soon everybody was petting my invisible rabbit again.

The requests to produce the invisible rabbit went on for a little while. Then our teacher took me aside. She was very nice, but my ability to bring out the invisible rabbit on request raised concerns that I did not know the difference between reality and fantasy.

As if I were talking to a stupid person, I explained the situation as best I could:

1. Yes, I know the difference between what is real and what is make-believe.
2. I do not have an invisible rabbit. I needed something for show and tell, so I used my imagination.
3. It makes the other kids happy to play with the rabbit, so I pretend to have it with me.

When word of this got back to my parents, my father thought the whole thing was hilarious. I would have forgotten about the incident, but it came back up years later. My mother was giving a handspinning demonstration at an arts festival. My friend Richie and I were left to roam the ground of the festival for the day.

Ritchie wound up working the bellows of a forge for a blacksmith. We were just little kids. Richie worked those bellows in the heat, smoke, embers, and flames for the whole day. He did such an incredible job that the blacksmith offered him an apprenticeship!

My day was spent with different artists. I spent time with a glassblower. I helped some archeologists excavate a site by a riverbank. After we dug and sifted some soil, they taught me how to throw a spear with an atlatl. Then I helped an organ grinder who let his monkey sit on my shoulder. I played a hammer dulcimer (poorly). A potter showed off what she called orgy cups, tried to explain what an orgy was (I already knew, I was playing dumb) before realizing she was talking to a seven-year-old boy (she made orgies sound a lot more interesting than throwing pots). I harassed a magician until he taught me a few tricks, and a clown tried to teach me how to tie balloon animals - but all of my poodles turned out looking suspiciously like knots and fists.

At first, my mother was beside herself. While Ritchie was working the forge like a man and learning a trade, I was off with the clowns and monkeys.

"He was off *playing*! His friend worked, and he played for the whole day!" Mom said in exasperation.

I could see her point, but while Richie was working like mad getting burned with sparks and his face blackened with soot, I was splitting my first-ever Chipwich between an organ grinder, the organ grinder's monkey and the magician.

On top of that, Richie learned to do one thing: pump the bellows at a forge.

Me? I walked away knowing how sculpt glass into a goldfish, perform a few coin tricks, learned how not to tie a balloon animal, discovered that a Chipwich is even better when you share it, promised myself to attend an orgy someday, found that monkeys are nowhere near as cute or clean as I imagined and that I could have taken down a woolly mammoth on my own. I would say that is a ton of useful knowledge!

My father calmed the situation down by saying, "Remember the rabbit?"

Mom nodded and let it rest.

Everything that happened after that often led my parents to reference either the invisible rabbit or the arts festival. They seemed to know in advance that the road I was destined to walk would be a different path from most.

Thankfully we walked much of it together — mom, dad, me and, whenever necessary, invisible rabbits.

The Guitar Girl

When the blind girl visited my classroom, I was sitting in the back, and I couldn't hear a goddamned thing.

Teachers usually stuck me back here where I was out of sight and bored out of my mind.

I could not hear. I have conductive hearing loss. I have had so many ear infections that my inner ear can no longer send sound waves to my auditory nerves.

As a child, all I knew was that my ears hurt, and people were hard to understand.

In Catholic school, the good sisters laughed at me for crying over a little earache. When mocking me didn't work, the nuns slapped me around.

I guess the Sisters of the Sacred Hearts of Jesus and Mary didn't buy into the whole suffer the little children part of the Bible back then.

Even when I switched to public school in the third grade, I was still stationed in the back of the class and ignored. My parents coached me to speak clearly. Being understood was useful in holding a conversation, but my teachers assumed that I could hear because I, as they eloquently put it, "didn't sound deaf."

I adapted to the situation. I taught myself to read lips and interpret body language. When my teacher realized I was reading her lips, she started covering her mouth with a sheet of paper.

My mother introduced me to literature. Jack London, H.G. Wells, Robert Frost, Carl Sandburg, Emily Dickenson, and Edgar Allan Poe quickly became favorites. I sat in school learning nothing and then went home and educated myself with stacks of books from the library. The librarians would get excited over the range of books I was devouring.

School days went by in a slow, silent crawl. The only break in the boredom was math. It made no sense to me. No matter how hard I tried, numbers got jumbled in my head. The only thing that was more bewildering than numbers was the way adults reacted to my difficulty. Teachers yelled or slapped me. My parents got angry. My Quaker tutor came scarily close to violence more than once.

It was a shame because I liked the tutor, but she really sucked at her job when faced with a student with a different perspective. Once she spread some coins on the table saying, "You have five coins. I take away two. How many do you have left?"

I counted the remaining coins. "One. . . Two. . . Three."

She slammed her hand on the table. The coins jumped. "No! Don't count it!"

"Then how do I know how many are left?"

"You should just know!"

I was trying hard not to swear. "How?"

Throwing her arms in the air, "You should just know!"

Mimicking her gesticulations, I yelled, "Jesus Christ!"

She put her hand on my copy of *A Tale of Two Cities*. "How can you read this and not understand math?"

"This is about the French Revolution!" It was my turn to slam the table. "The only math in the French Revolution was counting how many heads were in a pile!"

She held her head in her hands. Her boyfriend stepped in to end the session and make us all a cup of herbal tea.

Nowadays, they have a name for my trouble with math: dyscalculia.

I have trouble doing math in my head, difficulty with time, warped spatial relationships, and trouble with analog clocks. I can't remember names. I have no sense of the passage of time.

It should not have been a big deal. I did well in history, science, and English—but none of that mattered. Teachers told me to my face that my trouble with math stemmed from the fact that I was stupid, lazy, and stubborn.

Between teachers flipping out at me every math period and getting shuffled to the back of the classroom where I could not hear, I was a prime target for bullies. Most days saw some violence in my direction.

I learned the hard way that beating the crap out of a bully created a complex phenomenon. The defeated bully instantly became the victim, and they treated me like a monster. If I did not fight back, they labeled me a sissy. If I fought back and won, I would be a bad person. There was no way to win, so I just went crazy on any poor bastard dumb enough to pick a fight with me. If I lost a fight, I would start the fight again tomorrow or the next day until I won.

The day the blind girl visited my class, I felt alone. To the teachers and students, I was like an alien presence.

She came in with a guitar, led by her guide dog — a ray of light in a deeply dark place. Her long blond hair was brushed casually over her shoulder. She wore an unflattering striped top and a pair of red slacks. Her dog was a big German Shepard.

I don't know why the blind girl visited my classroom. The teacher said something that looked/sounded/read to my eyes and reached my one semi-functional ear as Lion's Club. I guess the local Lion's Club chapter had sent her.

I mostly ignored her presentation, and I hate to admit that I winced a bit when she broke out her Guild guitar. Then she said something that sounded like, "singalong."

Singalong? There was no way in hell the little monsters in my class would sing along. From my vantage point in the back of the room, I could see them giggling and making rude gestures.

Still, I drew myself up from my self-indulgent sulking slouch. I focused my eyes on her mouth and put together that the kids were to sing, "tick-tock, tick-tock" when she gave the signal.

Then she started to play, and I was never the same.

> My grandfather's clock was too large for the shelf,
> So it stood ninety years on the floor;

It was taller by half than the old man himself,
Though it weighed not a pennyweight more.
It was bought on the morn of the day that he was
born,
And was always his treasure and pride;
But it stopped short — never to go again —
When the old man died.

> Ninety years without slumbering
> **The kids**: *"tick, tock, tick, tock"*
> His life's seconds numbering,
> **The kids**: *"tick, tock, tick, tock"*
> It stopped short — never to go again —
> When the old man died.

In watching its pendulum swing to and fro,
Many hours he spent as a boy.
And in childhood and manhood the clock seemed
to know
And to share both his grief and his joy.
For it struck twenty-four when he entered at the
door,
With a blooming and beautiful bride;
But it stopped short — never to go again —
When the old man died.

> Ninety years without slumbering
> **The kids**: *"tick, tock, tick, tock"*
> His life's seconds numbering,
> **The kids**: *"tick, tock, tick, tock"*
> It stopped short — never to go again —
> When the old man died.

My grandfather said that of those he could hire,
Not a servant so faithful he found;
For it wasted no time, and had but one desire —
At the close of each week to be wound.
And it kept in its place — not a frown upon its face,
And its hands never hung by its side.
But it stopped short — never to go again —
When the old man died.

> Ninety years without slumbering
> **The kids**: "*tick, tock, tick, tock*"
> His life's seconds numbering,
> **The kids**: "*tick, tock, tick, tock*"
> It stopped short — never to go again —
> When the old man died.

It rang an alarm in the dead of the night —
An alarm that for years had been dumb;
And we knew that his spirit was pluming for flight
—
That his hour of departure had come.
Still the clock kept the time, with a soft and muffled
chime,
As we silently stood by his side;
But it stopped short — never to go again —
When the old man died.

> Ninety years without slumbering
> **The kids**: "*tick, tock, tick, tock*"
> His life's seconds numbering,
> **The kids**: "*tick, tock, tick, tock*"
> It stopped short — never to go again —
> When the old man died.

The kids sang along at every chorus. I was dumbfounded.

I watched her lead the children with gentle confidence. The teacher told us she was disabled, but with that guitar in her hands, she was so powerful. She could have been Artemis leading the hunt across the stars to Mount Olympus. I was in awe. I may have been in love.

With tears running down my eyes, I knew. I vowed. I promised myself with a knowing that went deep down to my bones that I would play the guitar someday. I would harness the power I had just witnessed.

Then one of my classmates saw my tears and laughed at me.

I got up and punched him in his face. Hard.

On the long slow walk to the principal's office, I pondered the magic of the guitar and the silly sad old song.

The vice-principal had a balding head beset with dandruff as flaky as a homemade pie crust. He had a misshapen goatee. He wore a worn brown blazer. He was not very intelligent. They had recently sent me to his office for fighting, and he menaced me with a spanking paddle. I asked him if he had two slices of bread. "Because if you touch me with that thing, I am going to make you eat it."

My dad was not happy over that call from the office.

Today the vice-principal was more interested in my tears rather than my reasons for punching the other kid. I would not have told this moron the truth for a million dollars. He would have done something cruel with the information.

Instead, with my eyes still damp with tears, I told him that the song made me sad about my grandfather.

"Oh. . . Did he, um, pass away?"

I gave a long pause before I answered with a cheesy grin. "No. He's just mean."

The joke did not go over well, but at least this time, my parents were not called. He yelled at me for a bit, and I just tuned him out. I sat there staring at him coldly, but inside I was thinking about that guitar and the sweetly gentle way she took those children and involved them in the song.

Deciding on my life's path was a big moment, but that decision did not factor in the difficulties I faced. Getting through to the adults in my life. Getting a guitar. Finding a teacher. Learning to play when I could hardly hear what people were saying to me. The list seemed insurmountable, but it couldn't be harder than math.

The rest of the day passed quietly. When I got home, I fished my harmonica out of my top dresser drawer. It was a Hohner Marine Band given to me by my mother the previous Christmas. When I held the instrument for the first time, mom told me, "This is music. If you have music, you can go anywhere in the world, and you will never be alone."

Now I understood her words. I had no idea how to play the harmonica, but I put the instrument to my lips and tentatively stumbled across the open notes to *My Grandfather's Clock*.

My grandfather's clock was too large for the shelf. . . It was clumsy, but the notes where there. It was a start.

That night I dreamed of guitars. It was not a dream where I was rich or famous. It was simpler and sweeter than that. I was sitting on a hill singing up to a starry sky, and people walking by stopped to sing along. I rarely remember my dreams. This one has stayed with me through these long years. It has comforted me when the going got rough.

The next day I started keeping my harmonica in my pocket so that I could practice anytime the chance arose. Someday I would have a guitar, and someday I would be able to play it. However long it took. Whatever it took.

I sometimes wonder what I would say or do if I met that guitar player today. How would I thank her? What would we play? Would I kiss her hands and thank her for showing me so gracefully that there was a way out—a way forward—that didn't involve apathetic teachers or fighting off bullies? Maybe we would not say much of anything at all and instead, sit on a hill singing up to the stars in the sky. Together.

The Core

Jenny stood in the living room of our home for as long as I can remember. She was all graceful curves and straight lines. Her wood glowing a deep amber that only comes with great age and heavy use.

Jenny is a Canadian spinning wheel. One of the first gifts my father bought for my mother.

Mom said that when she brought it home, her dad snickered behind his newspaper. As if he already knew that he would soon walk his daughter down the aisle.

Jenny had been carried across Canada and into America. She was used to spin so much wool that the impression of the original owner's foot was worn into the treadle.

My mother loved the old spinning wheel so much that she decided to take up handspinning. She was determined to learn how to spin. To use Jenny to spin wool into yarn.

When I was a child, it seemed that we were always looking for somebody willing to teach Mom how spin wool. We would load Jenny in the car and drive all over Pennsylvania. The trips always ended with Mom on the verge of tears. Nobody seemed willing or able to teach my mother how to spin.

Friends told Mom to give up, but she never quit. She continued her search for a teacher.

I had a hard time understanding why or how a teacher could turn somebody away. My mom said that there was a mystique to the process. If everybody knew how to spin wool, the current batch of hand spinners would no longer be unique.

I thought that was awful. Mom agreed, but what could we do about it?

Eventually, Mom found someone willing to sit with her. It only took a short time to get Jenny spinning. The first trick was to add a twist to the drive band. After that, Mom said everything fell into place.

Following that brief lesson, she was spinning wool into yarn with graceful ease. I would spend evenings carding loose wool into shape for spinning. Lanolin making my hands soft and slippery. Mom sang to the rhythm of the wheel. It was hypnotizing and beautiful.

When Mom started dyeing her homespun yarn, it was my job to go out into the woods to find natural dyes. I would wander into the woods of Chester County, Pennsylvania, and find the herbs that could turn Mom's yarn into glorious colors.

To this day, I can close my eyes and smell the dye pots and the scent of the wool yarn soaking in mordant. I can feel the heat and our laughter as we pulled dripping skeins of mom's yarn out of the cauldrons. Those were golden, golden days.

When I first took up the banjo, I made the mistake of forgetting the lesson of Mom's spinning wheel. I did not look for the core concept or technique that made bluegrass banjo work. I ended up confused and frustrated.

When I was twelve, my dad enrolled me in karate classes. My hearing made school difficult, and when you are different, it attracts bullies.

My grandfather tried to help me with the bully situation by teaching me how to fight. He was tougher than a cheap steak. Two guys mugged him when he was in his late seventies. He tied one mugger up with his belt. Then he tried to run over the second assailant in his car.

I put my grandfather's fighting tips to use against the bullies at school. I thought it would be over after a few fights, but for every bully I knocked down it seemed like two more popped up. The fights got crazy violent even after I tried everything to avoid conflict.

The first three martial arts academies I attended were rough places. Despite my young age, they often put me into sparring matches with adults. Dad was once waiting outside watching me train in a Tae Kwan Do school when he saw an adult walk up and kick me in the head hard enough to send me cartwheeling. As bad as it was, some moments were good, like the speed bag.

A speed bag is a little teardrop-shaped punching bag. You always see boxers hitting them like machine guns in Rocky movies. I tried like hell to make the speed bag work, but I was too slow—or so I thought.

One day a black belt saw me trying to hit the speed bag. He walked over and said, "let the bag do some of the work."

I looked at him like he was crazy, so he broke it all down for me into a simple formula:

1. Hit the bag. Let it swing back and hit the board. It will then rebound, swing forward and hit the board.

2. It will rebound again.

3. You hit it as it swings back from the rebound.

The pattern was punch–slap–slap. I was quickly able to work my speed up to what you see in boxing movies. People watching would say, "how does he do that?" I would show them, and they always said, "It can't be that easy!"

After three bad experiences and some injuries, we finally found a good karate school. This dojo taught American Kenpo, a system that incorporated elements of all the martial arts disciplines into one set of skills.

In the time I was studying Kenpo, we were not training for tournaments. We were training to fight.

I hate conflict. I don't want to fight, but Kenpo had a core set of skills that I honestly enjoyed practicing. I remembered Mom's spinning wheel as I threw myself into training. We had stances, blocks, punches, forms, and katas to learn. The handful of students that were my age constantly complained about how uncomfortable, difficult, and boring everything was. Most of them quit after a few weeks.

As I advanced in rank, it became clear that all the cool advanced stuff was built on or was an extension of the basic skills we learned at the very beginning.

By the time I was a blue belt, my instructors informed me that Ed Parker, the grandmaster of American Kenpo, was holding a workshop in Philadelphia.

I had heard about Ed Parker. I had read about his connection with people like Elvis and Bruce Lee, but I had never seen a photograph of the man. I imagined him looking like some guru from a karate movie. I was excited to have this chance to see him and learn from him.

We arrived at the workshop early. It was being held at a college gymnasium. The doors were all locked, so we just hung around in the parking lot.

It had not been a good trip.

My ride was one of the black belts at our dojo. He was really into the whole eighties' lifestyle. He stank of Brut cologne, and he drove a bright red convertible with a copy of Madonna's Like A Virgin album blasting from the tape deck. At red lights, people would stare at us while Pepe Le Pew fixed his moussed-up hair in the rear-view mirror. I did not think it was possible to be more embarrassed.

I would soon be proved wrong.

We arrived with my nose burning from drug store cologne, and my ears buzzing from songs like *Material Girl*, *Angel*, and (yecch) *Like A Virgin*.

We waited by the locked door. A large man cautiously approached us. He had gray hair, a bowl haircut and was wearing a Hawaiian shirt. He asked me if the door was locked.

I said, "Yes, it is. Nice shirt. Are you gonna sing *Nikki Hoi* or *Tiny Bubbles*?"

My ride punched me in the shoulder. Hard. I mean hard. "That is no way to talk to Ed Parker."

I froze and silently prayed for the earth to swallow me whole.

Ed Parker just chuckled and pretended I wasn't there while he chatted with the rest of the group waiting at the door.

I hoped and prayed that my faux paus would be forgotten, but during the workshop, Ed Parker said, "I need a volunteer."

Hands went up throughout the room.

I tried like hell to make myself invisible.

I kept my eyes down. When I brought them back up, Ed Parker was looking right at me. He pointed at me, saying, "You. The funny one."

Shit!

Long story short, Ed Parker used my fourteen-year-old body as a punching bag and a crash test dummy. He didn't hurt me too bad, but I will never cross a guy with a bowl haircut again.

Everybody got a good laugh at my expense.

It was okay. I had it coming.

After the seminar was over, my ride was talking with some friends. It looked like he was going to be a while, so I dragged my gear bag to the soda machine.

I decided something disgustingly sweet would cheer me up, so I got myself an orange soda. I took it outside and sat on the curb, swilling down sugar, unnatural dyes, and imitation orange flavoring. It was just what I needed.

"That stuff will kill you." I looked up into the smiling face of Ed Parker.

"I needed to wash the taste of my foot out of my mouth."

He got a laugh out of that.

"I am sorry about earlier," I said.

He waved my words away. "Don't worry about it."

He sat down on the curb next to me. "So, you are a blue belt. Are you training for your next belt test?"

I shrugged. "Sort of."

"Oh?"

"I go to the studio for class every night but Thursday. That's the night I go in and mop the floor so I can watch the black belts train."

"That's admirable."

I shrugged. "Not really. I don't have any friends, so I train."

"Have you thought about what you will do after Kenpo?"

"What do you mean *after* Kenpo? I'm taking this all the way I can. I want to open my own school someday."

"Things happen, Patrick. You never know where the road may take you. Just remember that what you have been taught in Kenpo can be applied to anything. Even music."

"I'll keep that in mind."

We talked for a little more.

I do not think I have ever been beaten up by a kinder or wiser man.

Ed Parker must have been psychic because a year later, my father and I were in a bad car accident.

I stopped training for a while, always planning to go back. Then I had an epileptic seizure, and that was that. Like Ed Parker said, Things happen.

Right after the car accident, I talked my dad into giving me a frailing banjo lesson. At this point in my life, my father and I did not see eye to eye much. We carried this lack of communication into the banjo lesson, which ended with Dad tearing the book we were using into confetti and throwing it into the air Rip Taylor style.

As Dad stomped away, he turned and said, "If you teach yourself how to play, I'll give you my new banjo. You won't do it because you don't pack the gear."

The next day I started training in the art of frailing banjo. From the notes dad brought home from his evenings with Paul the Beatnik and the little bit I got out of Dad before he gave up on me I saw that frailing banjo was all down-picking. The banjo is tuned to an open G major chord gDGBD. The lower-case g represents the fifth string.

The right hand:

- Ring and little finger lightly touch the palm.

- Middle finger is bent.

- Index finger is extended.

Sit up straight with the banjo pot flush against your belly.

Use a strap to support the weight of the instrument. Rest the middle fingernail of your right hand on the first (bottom) string and your thumb on the fifth (top) string.

Experiment with placement. Towards the bridge for a sharper tone or towards the neck for warmer tone. You can move from one position to another in the middle of a song!

Keep your right hand still. Use your forearm to raise your middle fingernail off the first string.

Drop your hand down, so the middle fingernail strikes the string sounding a note.

Raise your hand back up. Strum down across the strings with your middle fingernail.

At the end of the strum pop your thumb off the fifth string.

We now have three sounds. Strike, strum and thumb. This is the basic frailing strum. Everything you do with the five-string banjo is based on this technique. When you take it to the guitar, the pattern becomes a bass note, a chord, and an upstroke.

The same thing we hear all the time as boom shuck-a.

To win the bet with my dad, I played the basic frailing strum until our neighbors were ready to kill me.

I practiced in the morning and again at night.

I practiced walking up and down the driveway until the wee hours of the morning.

In Kenpo, we practiced relentlessly because our actions in combat must be instantaneous with no hesitation whatsoever. If you stop to think you get punched, stabbed, or worse. While it's cool to see fighters saying they will use such-and-such a punch in a movie, in real life there is no time. You act or you are a victim.

In music, we face a similar dilemma. As the music is happening, there is no time to think. You play or you fall out of rhythm and ruin the song for everyone involved. In order to act instinctively with the banjo or guitar, I had to practice the basics for an insane amount of time — three months to win the bet. Twenty years to get good.

A lot of modern students refuse to learn the basic skill set. They memorize melody lines, but when you rely solely on memory at a jam or performance, your brain will lock up. The music won't flow the way it does when two pickers sit down for a musical conversation. One complaint about the basics is that "it moves too slow!"

If talent truly existed (and I have yet to see it) music would not be worth the time or the effort. The fact that all of us are required to put in the same hard work to reach the same milestones is very inspiring to me.

People watch me play today and say, "It's easy for him because he has talent!" I get mad because my hearing made music harder for me than most. I can play today because I put my time in. I did the work, even on days when the muses were not being kind.

I did have one ally in my search for a way to get around my hearing trouble. My dad.

When I got good enough to start going to jam sessions, I found it nearly impossible because I could not make sense of the sounds all around me. I was nearly deaf, and the situation seemed hopeless. Hopeless, that is, until my dad switched from frailing a five-string banjo to strumming a tenor (four-string) banjo. Watching his strumming hand served as a sort of visual metronome.

So, there you have it. My teachers, a spinning wheel and the artist who made her work again. The karate master. My Dear Old Dad. To this day I am still parsing all the things I have learned from these people.

One: Identify the core skills.

Two: Practice relentlessly.

Three: Master one thing and you master other things.

Four: Let your friends help you.

One last thought: when you practice do not aim for perfection. Perfection is an impossible goal. Instead, think, "practice makes familiar." You are practicing something over and over so that you know it inside and out. When you need to call upon that skill, you will not hesitate.

Jenny still stands in our living room. We restored her to working order, so she has little antique value, but it's not like we would ever part with her. She is part of the family now.

Aunt Mannie

The cards began arriving so early in my life that I have no childhood memories without them. Every holiday without fail until my sixteenth birthday. Valentine's Day, Saint Patrick's Day, my birthday, Easter, The Fourth of July, Halloween, Thanksgiving, and Christmas. Always addressed in an old-fashioned way to Master Patrick Costello. Always with a few dollars tucked into the card and signed from my Aunt Mannie.

I did not get a lot of cards from relatives when I was a kid, so being able to rely on something in the mail every holiday meant a great deal to me. Even more so after my mother explained to me that Aunt Mannie was not really my aunt.

Her real name was Marion, and she was a cousin so distant that to this day, I still have a hard time grasping just how we were related. My mother knew Marion when she was growing up, and after I was born, Marion decided to start sending me cards on the holidays. Somewhere along the way, my mother and I started calling her my Aunt Mannie.

It is hard to put into words how it feels to be loved by somebody who has no obligation to do so. It warms the heart the way a fire in the hearth warms your hands and face.

When I was twelve, my mother took me on the long bus and subway ride across Philadelphia to visit Aunt Mannie for the first time. It was one of those perfect days in that space between Christmas and New Year's when the decorations are still up but the pressure of the holiday was over. After what seemed like an eternity of travel, we found ourselves at the front door of a little row house. We knocked, and Aunt Mannie answered the door.

She was a small woman, but not frail. She spoke in a flat Philadelphia accent. She wore an apron over her housecoat and a sweater over that.

Aunt Mannie hugged us and then rushed into the kitchen to make us some lunch. As she cooked, I looked around the place and slowly took the situation in.

My mother had explained to me a few times over the years that Aunt Mannie was poor, but until I walked into the house where she lived, I did not understand just how poor Aunt Manie really was. She was living with another one of my distant cousins. She had a room of her own, and that was about it.

It hit me that every card, every dollar tucked into those cards, and even the stamps represented a sacrifice this kind lady had made for me.

It was almost too much to process. I started to feel overwhelmed, but the next thing I knew Aunt Mannie was serving us the best dang grilled cheese sandwiches I have ever had and mugs of hot soup.

We enjoyed our lunch, and then it was time for us to start the long trip back home.

As we were leaving Aunt Mannie tucked a couple of dollars into my pocket. I tried to argue, but she just smiled and gently shoved me out the door.

Once I knew how to get to Aunt Mannie's place, I went to see her whenever I could. Sometimes I would just get disgusted with school and walk from Havertown all the way to 69th Street Station – usually dragging my guitar. If I didn't have any money, I would busk until I raised enough to take the Market-Frankford line to Aunt Mannie's. She never looked surprised to find me at her door.

We talked about many things in those visits. She even taught me how to make those perfect grilled cheese sandwiches. The only thing we did not talk about was the one question that nags me to this very day. Why me? Why sacrifice for so long for someone barely related to her? I once started to ask her, and she gently placed her cool hand on the side of my face for a moment before walking back into the kitchen to prepare more food.

The last time I saw her, I could tell something was wrong. As soon as I walked in, she got all excited about her new copper frying pan. I looked in the kitchen, and she was making grilled cheese sandwiches on a copper dustpan.

Before you ask, yes, I ate that sandwich. I couldn't bring myself to upset her. Sometimes loving someone requires accepting the occasional dust bunny in your lunch.

At her wake, my father walked with me to her coffin. I loved him for that. As we stood there, I asked him if he knew why she did so much for me.

Dad shrugged and said, "She loved you. No other reason than that."

I keep her picture on my desk. I think of her almost every day. Her example has influenced a lot of what I do as a teacher and as a human being.

Thank you, Aunt Mannie. I love you.

Paul the Beatnik

Growing up with childhood diabetes forced my father to develop an almost superhuman level of self-control. The man rarely loses his cool - making it even more shocking when dad came home from his first frailing banjo lesson completely freaked out.

He burst through the door, bellowing, "Soap! I need soap! I need to wash my hands! Twice! Three times! Jesus Christ! I feel so dirty!"

He dropped his banjo on the couch and rushed into the kitchen. As he washed his hands (three times), he went on to describe his evening.

"The House! It was the filthiest place I have ever seen! There is trash everywhere! The pets are all sick, and nobody ever cleans the cat box. It's a Mount Everest of turds, and you can see where the poor cat tried to climb the shit pile and fell off!"

I cracked up. I was sure that he was joking, but he kept going.

"We were playing our banjos, and there were fleas! Fleas! Fleas were hopping on my arm doing a fucking square dance!"

He pantomimed the little flea square dance on his arm.

"They had dinner. The dining room table had piles of trash on it, and they just threw the trash on the floor, and then after dinner, they piled the trash back on the table. I've never seen anything like it!"

I asked dad how the banjo lesson went.

"It wasn't really a lesson. We went over what I had taught myself from books. Then we went through a few songs. He wouldn't take any money for helping me."

I frowned. "Teaching for free? That's crazy."

"Well, he is a true Washington Square beatnik. He used to hang out with Bob Dylan and Dave Van Ronk."

"Cool."

"But the house!" Jesus Christ! It's the filthiest shithole I have ever been in! I have never seen anything like it!"

Dad went to wash his hands again and paused as he entered the kitchen. He cast a baleful glare upon me and raised his hand in the old Irish manner used alternately for casting a hex or letting a chump know not to mess with you. This time I think it was probably both.

"You are going to clean that pig-sty you call your room tomorrow. Then you will thank your mother for working so hard to make us a nice home to live in. Understood?"

"Sure, pop."

"UNDERSTOOD?"

"Yes! Yes! Okay!"

He was shaken up by this place, but he sounded enthusiastic about what Paul had shared with him. For the rest of the week, our house resonated with the sound of my dad practicing something he called basic frailing.

My father had been interested in the banjo for as long as I can remember. In high school, my dad played saxophone in the Monsignor Bonner high school marching band. At some point, he had been recruited to play his horn in a Mummer's string band.

The Philadelphia Mummer's Parade is the oldest folk parade in the United States. Every New Year's Day the Mummers march through the city with local clubs or associations competing in comic, fancies, string band, and fancy brigades.

My dad was a member of the Greater Overbrook String Band.

The Mummer's Parade began in the 18th century. Immigrant families began observing the European custom of visiting neighbors on Second Day Christmas, December 26th.

Over time this became a party that ran all the way through New Year's Day. Men marched from house to house firing guns in the air and pounding on doors demanding food and drink. They wore costumes, played instruments, fired guns (hence the modern term New Year's Shooters) and recited this rhyme at each house they visited.

> *Here we stand before your door.*
> *As we did the year before.*
> *Give us whiskey, give us gin.*
> *Open the door and let us in.*
> *Or give us something nice and hot.*
> *Like a steaming bowl of pepper pot!*

My father had a great time playing saxophone in the Mummer's Parade, but he couldn't help but notice that the banjo players were always having the most fun. While he was blowing his horn, the banjo players were singing, laughing, telling jokes and doing banjo player kinds of stuff. Dad promised himself that someday he would learn to play the banjo.

Then he met my mom. The banjo took a back seat to getting married and starting a family.

When I was almost seven, my dad came home with a Harmony five-string banjo. He signed up for Scruggs style banjo lessons because that was all the local music store offered. Then dad asked if I would like to take lessons with him. I was overjoyed! I didn't care about the banjo, but it was a chance to hang around with my father! I was ready to start picking. My enthusiasm lasted through a couple of lessons. I was okay with wearing fingerpicks. I was cool about practicing my rolls. My problem was that none of the music we were playing sounded very musical.

Scruggs style banjo, also known as bluegrass banjo or three-finger banjo, works by picking a constant string of eighth notes with the thumb, index and middle fingers of the (usually) right hand. The technique was popularized by Earl Scruggs, but it goes back to the very beginnings of the five-string banjo's development in North America.

Our bluegrass banjo teacher was a nice guy with an epic mustache and an insatiable craving for cigarettes. Lessons were held in a small room in the back of the music store. When I say small, I mean small like a broom closet but not as spacious. At every lesson, we were given exercises, rolls or songs, in banjo tab. The teacher would sit, smoke, and point to the tab as we played through it. There was no window, so the smoke would billow around the fluorescent light fixture in the ceiling and hang there in dull blue clouds. My eyes would burn. My throat would get sore. Worst of all, everything we played sounded the same. The basic rolls sounded like *Cripple Creek*.

Cripple Creek sounded just *like Foggy Mountain Breakdown.*

Foggy Mountain Breakdown sounded just like *The Beverley Hillbillies.*

We thought we were going crazy. How could all these songs sound the same? They had different chords. They had different melodies and lyrics. On the radio and television, they sounded different, but when we played them it was all the same.

When pressed, our teacher reluctantly explained that this approach to playing the banjo did not really work for singing folk songs on the front porch. Bluegrass was ensemble music and, as such, we would need a full band to fill out the sound and make our songs sound like songs. My father asked about alternatives. "What about the way Grandpa Jones played on Hee-Haw?" We were strongly advised to stay away from "that frailing stuff." We quit bluegrass and began searching for someone to help us learn frailing banjo.

The search for a teacher proved frustratingly difficult. We found some books on a modern approach to the old-time style called melodic clawhammer, but that stuff was as clueless as bluegrass. The clawhammer books focused completely on melody and discouraged singing in favor of playing all the notes a fiddle would play, but if we wanted to do that, we would have been learning the fiddle, not the banjo.

We sort of gave up for a while. Mom took up the dulcimer, and dad got heavily into black powder Pennsylvania flintlock rifles.

We started buckskinning, with all three of us camping period-correct for the fur trade era from about 1800 to the1840's. Mom wore prairie dresses, dad wore buckskins and I had a skunk skin cap. Our camp was a Sioux lodge. My bedroll was a Victorian silver tip grizzly pelt. I can't even begin to describe how wonderful it was drifting off to sleep in my father's tipi — snoring by the fire on that deep fur and watching the smoke roll up the lodge poles to the smoke flaps and out into the starry night sky.

It was a night like that at a rendezvous in the primitive camping area with probably a hundred other tipi's, lean-tos and tents that my father heard somebody playing Wildwood Flower on a five-string banjo. Dad rushed out to find the mysterious banjo player. Yes, the guy was frailing, but no, he would not help my dad learn the basics.

We had received a jolt of inspiration, but our search was far from over. Dad kept on trying, buying every book that he could find, but it was a few years before I found the poopy banjo man at the library.

Mom and I were at the Radnor library, just down the road from my father's hoagie shop. I was wandering around pulling books off shelves looking for something to read, hoping to find something, anything, that I had not already read.

There browsing the aisles was a man covered in horse manure with an equally crusty banjo slung over his back.

He had a filthy white beard yellowed with nicotine stains and long claw-like fingernails. I was excited about the banjo, but this guy was too funky even for me. I started to back away, but then my mother spotted him.

We approached him, and she encouraged me to ask if he played frailing banjo. He slung his banjo into playing position and broke out into *Cripple Creek* right on the spot. I told him that my dad would feed him lunch if he would stop by the hoagie shop and talk to us about frailing banjo.

He walked into the hoagie shop with me.

I think he was more excited about the free meal than talking about banjos with us, but he played a few tunes and invited dad to his place for a lesson.

Now the first lesson was over, and dad was still washing his hands.

After that, dad started visiting once a week and every week we learned something else about our new friend. His name was Paul. His back story changed depending on who asked. He was a blacksmith, an antique clock restoration expert, a jewelry maker, a banjo builder/repairer and a dizzying number of other obscure trades. He could do a lot of things, but he would not work if possible.

My grandfather said that Paul was the laziest man he had ever met - and went on to add that if Paul shit himself in bed, all he would do is kick the turds out from under the blankets and go back to sleep.

I thought that was a horrible thing to say about anybody, but I could not argue that it wasn't true.

Paul lived with a lady named Kitt, and she was the one who opened the house to the growing group of musicians that became The Wednesday Night Banjo and Donut Marching Society that started with my dad, and then me.

I did not go with my dad for his first few visits, and I thought that he had been joking or exaggerating when he described the condition of the house. Then I finally tagged along. It was so much worse than he had described.

I had read about hoarders in books, but this was my first encounter with such a household. There was stuff everywhere. Some of the clutter was valuable antiques, and some of it was garbage. In addition to stuff, Kitt also collected strays. Stray dogs. Stray cats. Even stray people. Week to week, it was hard to tell how many folks were living in the place.

My first visit I had the bright idea of bringing Chinese food to share with our hosts. As dad had told me, the trash on the dining room table was thrown on the floor in order to clear space for the meal. We passed around various containers of Chinese food, and there was more than enough for everyone. When I was finished, I dumped my scraps into the trash. As I carried my plate to the overloaded sink, Paul ran to the trash can. To my horror, he fished out my spare rib bones and started gnawing on the leftover gristle. He saw the poleaxed look on my face and shrugged.

"You'll do the same if you play long enough."

"No. I don't think so."

While I have had a lean moment or two in the years since then, I have yet to gnaw on spare rib bones out of the bin.

Like dad said after his first visit with Paul, he never really taught us much. He helped clarify a few concepts, but most weeks we just killed time together. Paul did introduce me to Peggy Seeger and Elizabeth Cotton, but at the time he was only trying to get himself invited to an after-concert party. When I wound up getting a banjo lesson from them instead, he was a little bit put out.

That was the hard part of being friends with Paul. His values were so different from ours that it sometimes left our heads spinning. The one-time dad took Paul's advice on buying a banjo two things happened:

- Dad overpaid for a vintage banjo that had been junk when it was new.
- Paul got a kickback.

To this day I don't understand. If he needed money, he could have simply asked us, and we would have happily given him what we could. He knew that, but he set dad up anyway. I just don't understand.

Eventually, the Wednesday Night Banjo and Donut Marching Society drifted apart. We stayed in contact with Paul, but he moved out of Kitt's house, and we moved to Maryland.

In the early 90's we got word that Kitt was sick. We drove up to see her at her home. A few months later, we heard that she was in hospice care. We took our banjos and my guitar to play for her. We sang one of her favorite songs, *The Saint James Infirmary Blues* before I noticed that this was not the right venue to sing:

> *I went down to see her doctor.*
> *She was very low he said.*
> *I went back to see my baby.*
> *Great God, she was dead.*

Kitt loved it. Before we left, my dad leaned close to Kitt. He thanked her for opening up her home to us and told her that we loved her.

We got word soon after that she was gone.

By that point, dad and I were professionals. We could play anywhere with anybody. We took Paul's example of teaching for free and took it to the internet. The last time I talked to him he said it was a crazy way to do business. A lot of replies came to mind, but I just said that we were sharing the way he and other teachers had shared with us.

"Times change, Patrick." He said.

"Only if you accept the changes," I said.

Tiny

The hot August sun shone in the impossibly blue Summer sky like God was holding a fistful of diamonds. The grass under my feet was deep green and freshly cut. The scent was mixing with the Chester County honeysuckle and the sharp odors of the rich forest surrounding the field.

This was my first visit to Old Fiddlers' Picnic, but I already felt as if I was coming home.

The festival used to be held at Lenape Park. Just a stone's throw from my grandfather's summer cabin on the Brandywine Creek. I grew up with stories of my mother learning to dance at Old Fiddlers' when she was young and enjoying the music with my father when they were courting. Lenape Park had closed, and now the gathering was being hosted by Chester County at Hibernia Park.

I had been playing frailing banjo just a few months after taking up the instrument to win a bet with my dad. Now I was here. I knew a few songs, and I realized that I was desperate to learn more. Mom, dad, and grandpop were busy setting up our picnic spot.

I looked down the hill, and the sheer number of people making music made my head spin. I felt like an extra in one of those old cast of thousands epic motion pictures.

I really wanted to go out and try to jam with everybody I could, but I only knew a couple of chords and a few songs. I would have to be crazy to go down there. So off I went.

I slung my banjo over my shoulder, wiped my sweaty palms on my jeans, and strutted out among the pickers like I was ten feet tall. At first, I stayed to myself. I just stood on the outskirts of the different jam sessions and tried to look knowledgeable. Some of the old-timers seemed to know right away that I was full of shit, but they didn't give me a hard time. I got all the way down to the food concessions before somebody called my bluff.

"What have you got, kid?" said a gruff voice from behind me.

I turned around. A very large man with a battered National guitar was towering over me. His eyeglasses were dark so that I couldn't see his eyes. A hat was pushed back on his bald head. His face was framed with heavy jowls. A fat cigar was sticking from the corner of his mouth. The cigar smoke curled around his head like a cloud stinking to high heaven.

I stared at his guitar in wonder. National guitars were-and still are-made from brass or steel. This one was steel, probably made in the 1920s. The strings went over an aluminum cone to create an amplified tone in the days before the electric guitar.

The location, the man and the guitar came together into the coolest thing I had ever seen.

"What have you got?" he asked again, jolting me from staring.

I held out my banjo. "A banjo!" I said.

Even though his dark glasses, I could tell he was rolling his eyes.

"I know that, you little dipstick. You think somebody as old as I am never saw a banjo before? I'm asking you, 'what have you got?' Play something!"

As green as I was, I could see thousands of hours of music etched all over that National guitar. I started thinking up excuses so I could get out of playing for the old man.

He must have seen the fear on my face because he shook his head in disappointment and started to walk away. I realized that I was letting an important moment slip through my fingers. I was blowing It. Stupid! My hands shaking from nerves and adrenaline, I grabbed my banjo and tore into the best song that I knew: *The White House Blues*.

The old man stopped and cocked his head towards my banjo. He slowly turned around and watched me ruin a perfectly good song. After I played it through once, he didn't tell me to stop, so I ran through it again. I thought he smiled, but I wasn't sure. His face was shrouded with his sunglasses and a halo of cigar smoke.

He still didn't tell me to stop, so I kept going, and as I played, he waved some of his friends over.

I was quickly surrounded by old men carrying battered guitars and mandolins. A lot of them wore baseball caps. Some of them had slacks going up practically to their armpits.

"What's the kid playing?"

"Sounds like *White House Blues,* but the kid is so scared he's playing too fast."

"Ain't no kid knows that song."

"Where did he learn to play the old-time banjo?"

"It's been a long time since I heard that."

More was said, but I couldn't pick it all up. Being almost deaf, I learned to read lips at an early age. Through it all, the big guy with the cigar and the National guitar just watched me and smoked. As I finished, he said something that made his buddies laugh out loud, but I missed it. Probably a good thing.

After I had finished the song, the circle of old-timers that had gathered around me cheered and patted me on the back.

"Not bad kid!" somebody said.

The big guy with the cigar and the National guitar didn't say a thing. He just watched me for a moment, and then he began to play his guitar. I knew the melody right away. *The White House Blues*.

He nodded to a fiddler in the group, and soon the fiddle was carrying the melody while he chopped chords on the guitar. Then a mandolin joined in, and soon the whole group of old-timers was playing and singing *The White House Blues* a whole lot better than I had played it.

They *owned* that song. Ran through it as familiar as you walk through your living room. After a while, the man with the National guitar gave a signal, and they all ended at the same time, just as sweet and easy as you please.

I had a million questions, but I was so blown away that all I could say was "Wow!"

The old man with the National guitar waved me close and showed me a couple of licks. Some of the other old-timers had tips for me. All of them wanted me to slow down. A mandolin player chopped out the chords to the song slowly while a guitar strummed along as I tried to play the melody.

They told me to stop worrying about mistakes and keep my rhythm steady at all costs.

"It's the rhythm, kid. That's got to stay the same no matter what happens."

Then the old man nodded to his pals. That must have been the signal that our impromptu lesson was over. He said, "Okay now, get lost. Go and work on that. Don't come back until you can do like we showed you." Then they started to walk away.

I wanted to thank them. I wanted to follow them. I started after them, but National Guitar Guy shot me a look that I knew from my time studying karate. I was not welcome. I had not yet earned my place in the circle.

"How will I find you again?"

"Come to the festivals. Ask for Tiny."

"I'm Patrick."

"Get lost, Patrick."

I ran back up the hill just as fast as my feet would carry me. I couldn't wait to get home, practice, and earn my place in the jam with Tiny and his pals.

A month later, my father took me to my second fiddle festival. This one was in Lyons, Pennsylvania near Kutztown. We arrived early, but Tiny was already there. He was sitting on a tree stump playing his National guitar.

I was so excited to introduce him to my dad. Then I made sure to show him that I had been working on the licks he had shown me with his friends. Tiny seemed happy with my progress, but he told me that the real test is getting on the stage.

"On stage? I just started!"

"That's no reason!"

Once again, I knew from my experience in karate that you could train your heart out and it won't mean a thing if you never step into the ring. Tiny was right. I had to get on stage somehow.

I thought about telling dad, but I knew he would say no. I had to make something happen. I did what I do best. I waited for an opportunity to present itself.

After many hours of happy music-making in the hot Pennsylvania sunshine, I managed to slip away from dad to bullshit the stage manager. I told him that my father and I were big-time banjo experts on our way home from a gag.

"Gag?" He looked at me incredulously. "You mean, 'gig' don't you?"

"We call them gags now in Nashville. Try to keep up with the lingo."

The stage manager was going to run me off, but somebody said, "Put him on. The kid's got guts."

I turned around. Tiny was smiling at me.

The stage manager sighed. "Okay. He's on in fifteen minutes."

Fifteen minutes? I started to panic. I still had to tell dad. I started to say something, but Tiny squeezed my shoulder gently and said, "don't push your luck." I was off like a shot to find my father.

I found him as he was stepping out of the restroom.

"Dad! We're on in fifteen minutes!"

A look of black seething rage flashed across my father's face. He took a deep breath. Then he smiled at me and said, "well, we better get ready."

I was still a rank beginner.

All I could play was, *The White House Blues*, *Boil Them Cabbage Down*, some of *Wildwood Flower* and *Wreck of the Old 97*. We ran through the three and one-half songs that I knew a few times, and then it was time to head for the stage.

It was only then that I realized how massive the audience was. There were a couple of thousand people in the field.

The stage was a flatbed trailer decorated with hay bales. We climbed the rickety steps and looked over the microphones at the sea of people. In a wild flash of realization, I understood that as scared as I was, every person out in the audience wished they were me. Standing with my dad. My best friend.

Dad smiled at me and said, "I don't know where we're going, but we are on our way!"

Then we walked up to the microphones and did our thing.

The audience cracked up when dad told them about being told he was going on stage with no notice. Then we played our songs. I was too scared to tell if we were doing good or bad, so I assumed the worst.

My legs were shaking, and sweat was pouring in my eyes, but I kept on playing and singing.

Then it was over. We got a lot of applause. We stepped off the stage and some of the bluegrass musicians we had admired earlier in the day rushed towards us, asking where we had learned to play old-time banjo. I felt ten feet tall.

I turned to Tiny. He said we were awful, but that was okay because we had the guts to get on stage. We would do better next time and the time after that.

As I was leaving, Tiny said we would jam at the next festival. My father and I were part of the group now.

I saw Tiny a handful of times after that. I never knew his real name. When I started playing guitar, I got a shiny Dobro 33H. I played my Dobro all over Philly smoking cigars and trying to be as cool as Tiny.

I wrote my first book twenty years after first meeting Tiny. I started with the question that changed my life.

"What have you got, Kid?"

Tiny taught me that you can have a huge impact on a person simply by being willing to share. To lay down a challenge. "Don't come back until you can do like I showed you." It was gentle pressure that forced me to become a better musician.

I do not know his name, but Tiny left thumbprints all over my music that remain to this day. His kindness inspires me to this day.

I know in my heart that we will see each other again. When we do it won't be a big deal. We will compare wear and tear on our resophonic guitars, smoke a stogie, and play some sweet music. Just as if we saw each other yesterday.

Maybe by then, I will be half as good a guitar player as Tiny. Maybe not.

Thank you, Tiny. I love you.

Enter the Dobro

I was sitting on our back steps smoking cigars and trying to play a guitar I had fished out of a trash can.

The guitar was junk. Somebody had gotten frustrated or had been trying to emulate The Honky-Tonk Man on WWF wrestling and smashed it to pieces. The entire lower bout was broken, and there was a large hole in the back like somebody gave the instrument a swift kick.

It may have been crap, but it was still a guitar! For years I had dreamed of becoming a guitar player, but my dad was convinced that I did not pack the gear. He said the guitar was too difficult, and that every kid in Philly has a guitar gathering dust in the closet. Everybody wants to play the guitar, but very few are willing to put in the time and effort it takes to learn.

My father did see that I was getting better with the banjo, and helping me satisfy my burning desire to be like old Tiny with his National resonator guitar, he purchased a Dobro banjo for me. This instrument had the wood body of a resonator guitar with a five-string banjo neck. The strings went over an aluminum cone inside the body to make the instrument ring with rich tones. It wasn't very loud, but it looked cool and sounded even cooler. Everywhere I went with my Dobro banjo people wanted to jam with me and talk about Dobro and National instruments. I almost forgot about the guitar, right up until Roger came along.

Roger was an almost-famous banjo player. He played bluegrass and frailing banjo better than anybody, but he never quite managed to get as famous as he thought he should be. Because of this and probably other things, Roger got mean. I would run into him two or three times a year, and I always walked away so mad that I would practice endlessly so that I would be stronger the next time we met.

When I got my Dobro banjo, I was so excited to show it to Roger. I was convinced that this instrument would help me start a real conversation with him.

He was such a good musician. I really wanted to learn from him.

Alas, it wasn't to be. Roger took one look at my Dobro banjo and frowned. "Why don't you get a real banjo?"

I tried to laugh it off and get the group jamming. After a few songs, Roger said, "Play that thing like a banjo or a guitar. You can't be both. It's distracting. Make up your mind."

As much as it pained me to admit, Roger was right. I wasn't frailing my Dobro banjo. I was wearing picks and playing rolls I had picked up from guitar players. As much as I loved my Dobro banjo, it was neither guitar nor banjo. I had to choose one and stick to it or get my grubby mitts on a guitar. Rather than scheme like a kid hoping for a Red Ryder BB gun for Christmas, I put my fate onto the drifting currents of the Tao. If I was supposed to be a guitar player, God or the universe would find a way to put an instrument in my hands.

Not long after that, I spotted the smashed guitar in the trash.

If my trashcan find had been a steel-string guitar, I would have left it. Steel-string acoustic guitars are engineering marvels. The wooden box of the guitar body is under immense strain from the tension of bringing steel wire strings to concert pitch. Luckily, I had found a classical guitar.

Classical guitars evolved from baroque instruments strung initially with gut. Modern classical guitars use nylon strings. It takes much less force to bring nylon strings to concert pitch. This meant that I would be able to make the trashcan guitar playable with Elmer's glue, popsicle sticks, and duct tape.

Lots and lots of duct tape.

In the space of an afternoon, I finally had a guitar of my very own. I did not care that it smelled like expensive cheese and looked like cheap junk. I finally had a guitar! Now I had to learn to play the damned thing.

We had a couple of folk song anthologies in the house, and most of them had basic guitar chords. I sat down on the back steps and started twisting my fingers to make chords for the keys of G major and C major.

On the five-string banjo, we play out of open tunings, and the chord shapes are easy except for the F major chord. That one is a bitch. I was confident as I sat down and prepared to put my fingers on the fretboard to make the G major chord.

I placed my ring finger on the first string at the third fret. Okay, not too bad. Next, I had to reach across the fretboard and grab the sixth string at the third fret. Holy Shit! I felt like I was reaching across the Grand Canyon! To finish the G major chord, I fretted the fifth string at the second fret with my index finger.

Recap G major chord:

- First string at the third fret.

- Fifth string at the second fret.

- Sixth string at the third fret.

All of that to make a G major chord? No wonder everybody quit! I strummed the chord and it was awful. It took me hours to get my hand and fingers in place to fret the chord cleanly. Then it was time to work on the C major chord. Second string at the first fret, fourth string at the second fret and the fifth string at the third fret.

Recap C major chord:

- Second string at the first fret.

- Fourth string at the second fret.

- Fifth string at the third fret.

Once I could play the G major and C major chords I had to choose between the D major or the F major chords. Everybody I knew said the F chord was the worst, so I decided to tackle that one next. To form an F major chord I had to grab the first and second strings at the first fret, the third string at the second fret, the fourth string at the third fret and reach around the guitar neck with my thumb to fret the sixth string at the first fret.

Recap F major chord:

- First and second strings at the first fret.

- Third string at the second fret.

- Fourth string at the third fret.

- Sixth string at the first fret.

The G major chord had been a challenge.

The C major chord had been downright hard.

The F major chord kicked my ass.

The F chord was so hard and so difficult that I started wondering if maybe somebody was playing a joke on me, that tomorrow a television host would jump from the bushes telling me that the F major chord in all my books had been made intentionally hard by some mean bastard.

As time went on, I started to understand why such a hard chord form has become the default F major chord. It was a shared hardship. No matter where you go in the world, you will have the common bond of mastering the bloody agonizing chord of death. All guitar players, regardless of genre or style, have endured the days of trying to force their fingers to form an F major chord.

Making chords is only part of the battle. The next step is to sing songs while strumming the rhythm on guitar and changing chords for harmony. Even songs as familiar as *Happy Birthday* in the key of C will require that you sing while running through the C, F and G chords – and you have to put your fingers in the right position to make the chords without a moment of hesitation.

I quickly realized that my dad might have been right. I could not do this. I would be better off sticking to the banjo, but then I thought about Tiny with his National resophonic guitar. I wanted to be that cool.

So, I rubbed my sore hands, cracked my knuckles, and went back to practicing that God-cursed F major chord.

I told myself that it would get better with practice. It took me two weeks to teach myself a few songs on my trash-can guitar.

I was feeling cocky, so I went with my dad to The Wednesday Night Banjo and Donut Marching Society, a loose band of banjo students that met at Paul and Kitt's house. Everybody was surprised to see me playing and singing with my stinky guitar. By the end of the jam, somebody offered to loan me a nice old Epiphone if I would give up the trashcan guitar.

Everyone seemed to be afraid it was going to give me tetanus or something.

The Epiphone was a great guitar, but it did not belong to me. That meant I couldn't drag it all over Hell's half-acre like I did my banjo. It also meant I couldn't take it with me to school — or cut school if you know what I mean.

I knew it was foolish to complain. I guess the truth of it was that the guitar took everything I had to play at a basic level. To work so hard on a guitar I did not own was frustrating. Frustration has its good points. My hearing was almost gone by the time I got serious about the guitar. I could hear my banjo because banjos are louder than awkward gas-passing at a job interview. The guitar was nearly silent to me. In frustration, I laid my cheek against the upper bout of the instrument. When I strummed the strings, I could hear the guitar!

I had discovered bone conduction. I have conductive hearing loss. That means my inner ear is not working, but my auditory nerves were/are just fine. By resting my cheek —and later my teeth — on the guitar, sound waves traveled through my skull to my auditory nerves allowing me to hear my guitar! As I was working on all this guitar stuff, my schoolwork went out the window. My family was not happy about this. I was trying to play a blues song out on the back steps. My dad came out. He was eating an apple.

(bite-chew) "What are you doing?"

"I'm playing the blues, dad."

(bite-chew) "That's not the blues." He paused, took another bite of his apple, and looked like he was searching for the right word. He smiled. "That's shit."

He laughed and went back inside. I sat there with a borrowed guitar that I had to use my teeth to hear. I wanted this more than anything, and nothing was working out. I sat there and cried for a while. Then I put my teeth on the upper bout and went back to work. Deafness, epilepsy, crappy guitars and the awful F major chord were not going to get the best of me. I was going to play the guitar. Nothing was going to stop me.

The next day my dad woke me up early. It was his day off, and he said we were going to take a ride. I got in the truck with him. Dad said, "let's go get you a real guitar." Being Irish and Pennsylvania Dutch and Catholic, I tried to tell my dad that I did not need a new guitar. He called bullshit on that, and we were on our way.

"Where are we going, pop?"

"I put a lot of thought into this. We're going to Mandolin Brothers."

I just about shouted for joy. Mandolin Brothers, at that time, was the single most fabulous music store on God's green earth. They carried the rarest and most desirable acoustic fretted instruments ever made. As excited as I was, there was also a knot of nerves in the pit of my stomach. Guitars at Mandolin Brothers ran from a few hundred bucks to hundreds of thousands of dollars. How was I going to know what to buy? How could I get a good guitar without breaking the bank? As we drove from Philadelphia to Staten Island, I told myself to stop worrying. Let the Tao take me where I was supposed to go and focus on this once in a lifetime trip with my best friend. We got to Mandolin Brothers before the store opened. My dad feels like he is late unless he is an hour early.

While we waited for the store to open, Dad asked me what I was looking for in a guitar. Right away I told him I wanted a resonator guitar like Tiny played, but I was quick to add that it was unlikely because vintage National guitars were crazy expensive at that time. There was a company making new metal-body resophonic guitars, but I did not know where to get one. Dad asked me about Martin or Gibson guitars. I shrugged. "I guess they are okay." The front door of Mandolin Brothers opened. We climbed out of dad's truck and went into the store.

Walking into Mandolin Brothers was surreal. You stepped into the area where the actual business of the store was conducted. Stan Jay set up his workstation this way so that he could greet every customer, and he did just that when we walked in. He welcomed us to the store and told us not to be afraid to pick up and play any instrument on display. He shook our hands and then, like Willy Wonka, escorted us to a room pulled from the imaginations of his customers. Everywhere you looked, there were *wonderful* things. Guitars, ukuleles, banjos and then I saw it.

In one of the little rooms set off from the main display floor, hanging on the wall bathed in a ray of early morning sunshine much like Jake Blues in the chapel when he was sent on a mission from God, was a metal-body guitar that was bigger and badder than Tiny's old National. The moment I saw it, I knew that this was my guitar. Before I went to look closer at the beautiful and mysterious metal-body resophonic guitar I did the normal guitar shopper thing and tried a few vintage and new Martin guitars; then I did the same with some Gibson guitars. I didn't want to run the risk of chipping or drooling on the finish, so I skipped the bone conduction trick. Instead, I just strummed a simple rhythm while holding a C major chord to get a sense of how these instruments felt in my hands. Somebody working the counter noticed that I was playing the same chord over and over. He came over and asked me if I even knew how to play the guitar.

"Well, I know how to play a C chord."

"Okay. . . but do you know anything else?"

"No, but I can play the hell out of a C chord."

The counter guy made a face and left me alone.

After that, dad and I had one of our silent conversations. It's almost like sign language only with looks and facial expressions instead of hand gestures.

> **Dad:** "Okay. He really was a weenie."
> **Me:** "Yup."

Eventually, I could put it off no longer. We went into the room with the resophonic guitars on display. The instrument that had caught my eye was a Dobro model 33 Hawaiian. The hangtag also called it a bottleneck special, perfect for playing slide, country blues and anything else you could imagine. It was a massive guitar and, unlike Tiny's National, this guitar was made from bell bronze rather than steel. It had a maple neck that had all the grace of a two-by-four compared to the other guitars I had played that morning, but you needed a heavy neck to balance out the weight of the chrome-plated bronze body. I was in love. I looked at the price tag: twelve hundred dollars. Holy shit! Nope! Danger Will Robinson! Danger!

As much as I wanted – needed this guitar, there was no way in hell I was going to stick my dad with that price tag.

"That looks cooler than Tiny's guitar," Dad said.

"Yeah, but it's too much. They have a plywood Dobro for a lot less."

"Plywood? You'll never play it."

"But dad. . ."

"If you buy the cheap guitar, it's going to let you down. You won't practice. You won't progress. You won't learn." He pointed to the 33H. "That is your guitar!"

Dad went to get a sales rep to help us take the Dobro 33H down so that I could give it a whirl and maybe try the bone conduction trick. Dad came back with a guy, and he would not take the Dobro down unless we agreed to let him fit me with a more traditional acoustic guitar. I didn't want to be a dick, so I reluctantly agreed. He came back with the same guitars I had checked out earlier. Dad went to get another salesman.

The second sales guy was also reluctant to put the Dobro in my hands. Instead, he decided to play it for me. Again, I was polite up to a point, but after a while, I started getting mad. Was this guitar on hold for a friend? Defective? Were these guys screwing with us? I could not pin down exactly what was happening, but it was clear that they did not want to sell me this guitar.

Dad sensed my growing frustration. He went and got Stan Jay. Stan, thank God, finally handed me the Dobro, but even he started rattling off reasons I should not buy this guitar. I looked Stan in the eye.

"Do you want to sell this guitar or not?"

Stan left me alone with the Dobro at last.

I strummed a chord. The vibrations from the strings transferred to the maple bridge, to the aluminum cone under the bridge and filled the room like a pipe organ in a cathedral. On top of that, the bronze body vibrated allowing me to feel the bass in my chest. I leaned forward and rested my cheek on the upper bout as I strummed. My head filled up with musical fireworks.

Dad watched me the whole time.

"Well?"

"It's a great guitar, dad, but it's too much money."

"Let me worry about that."

I started to argue, but dad pointed out that he couldn't buy me my first car because of my epilepsy. He could, however, buy me my first good guitar. I got choked up. I stood there in the greatest guitar shop in the world receiving one of the greatest gifts a father ever gave a son with tears running down my face.

As Stan was tracking down the case for my guitar and writing up the bill, Dad went back into the shop and got a National guitar for himself. His guitar is a 1928 tenor meaning it has four strings and you play it like a tenor or plectrum banjo. "In for a penny, in for a pound," said my dad. We drove home buzzing with excitement. Mom and grandpop looked at us like we were crazy, but I did not expect them to understand.

My Dobro 33H is more than just a guitar. It is a promise from my dad that he believed in me when I gave him almost no reason to do so.

The Dobro also created opportunities for me. Old pickers would see me sitting on a curb smoking a cigar and strumming this big shiny guitar, and they had to walk over to find out more about me. The Dobro was also perfect for my bone conduction trick. I could practice for hours with my teeth resting on the upper bout of the guitar so that the sound waves could travel through my skull to reach my auditory nerves. It filled my head, heart, and mind with music, love for my dad, and fear of the mighty F major chord.

The finish is worn off the neck of my Dobro 33H now. The chrome is still in pretty good shape, but there is a big dent shaped just like my big toe. The guitar is so heavy that my strap broke, sending the instrument crashing down directly on my big toe like a watermelon falling on a grape. The guitar has other scars, and each one has a story. Some of the stories are fun to share and others. . . Well, some are best kept between me and my guitar.

When I ran up to Tiny with my Dobro, he nodded in approval but cautioned me that if I carried this guitar around, people would eventually expect me to be able to play it.

I wrestled with the evil F major chord and, over time, started to make sense of the fretboard. I was lucky to meet guitar players who were willing to share with me. Best of all, I got to sit with my dad — he with his National tenor and me with my Dobro 33H. We made music together on the front porch, on stage, on television, and on the radio.

Heck, the book you are reading right now is another adventure I am having with my dad.

Sometimes I stop and wonder, "What if."

What would have happened if I had never pulled that battered guitar out of the trash?

What would have happened if I had given up when I realized how hard it would be to learn the guitar?

What would have happened if I had backed away from buying the Dobro?

The answer?

Nothing would have happened. Nothing at all.

Why I Play the Banjo

It started while I was eating breakfast. I was in my room enjoying my meal when the room started to spin. Then everything went black. The world seemed to rush back at me, and I was. . . Well, I did not know where I was.

As I opened my eyes, I winced at the bright lights overhead. I could feel rather than hear a lot of people milling around, and my nose was lightly burned by the smell of antiseptic.

I was in a hospital emergency room. Something bad had happened. I racked my brain and only got a few unusual images in place of recollection. I realized that my hand hurt like hell. I looked down, and a nurse was trying to start an IV in the back of my left hand. She was doing a bad job. She had stuck me several times, and I was bleeding heavily. Blood trickled down my fingertips to a growing pool on the floor. I tried to sit up, and my entire body groaned in protest. Everything hurt. It felt like I had pulled every muscle and sprained every joint. Even my hair hurt.

A dim memory flashed across my mind of my grandfather picking me up off the floor and wiping my face with a gentleness I did not know he had in him. He said, "Oh Patrick, what am I going to do with you?"

What the hell had happened to me?

I tried to talk to the nurse, but she ignored my questions. The longer things went with nobody talking to me, the scarier my situation got. Eventually, the nurse gave up tearing at my hand and started trying to stick the needle in my wrist. It hurt like hell. I asked her if she was digging for truffles. She left in a huff and came back with an older nurse who also would not talk to me other than to say, "Stay still!"

When you are fifteen, you feel invincible right up to the moment things get out of control. I had been in hospitals before, and my karate instructors taught me how to stay composed even when I was getting my ass kicked. I tried to meditate and stay calm until somebody would tell me what was happening.

I fell asleep. I woke up as they were prepping me for a CAT scan. There were a lot of doctors and nurses involved with getting me ready, and they were all talking at once. Things got fuzzy again.

I woke up in a semi-private room. The curtain was drawn around my roommate's bed. My half of the room had a TV, a couple of chairs and a bedside table with an ashtray and a book of matches. (It was the 1980s, folks. You could smoke in hospitals back then).

I still had the IV in my arm. Whatever they were pumping into my veins was making the muscles in my arm cramp up. I looked around the room for some clue as to how I had gotten here. No dice. After what seemed like an eternity, a doctor strolled in and informed me he was my neurologist. He coldly explained that I had just experienced a grand mal seizure — a sort of short circuit in the brain that triggered convulsions. The medicine in the IV was called Dilantin. I told him I read about Dilantin in

One Flew Over the Cuckoo's Nest a long time ago. He didn't seem to care.

He informed me I was probably never going to drive a car or hold a regular job. He added that I would be on medication for the rest of my life. He was coldly and disturbingly disinterested and left before I could gather myself together enough to ask questions.

I thought I could hear my roommate cursing on the other side of the curtain, but I wasn't sure.

I fell back onto my pillow. Epilepsy? As in Julius Caesar? I was already almost deaf and now God is shaking my brain like a kid mixing sea monkeys? I felt absolutely alone.

My folks came to see me. My grandfather was raising hell that I didn't have "No God-damn epy-lepsy." He swore that my problem stemmed from running around in my bare feet and eating baked beans out of the can. We all got a laugh out of that, but we were all scared out of our wits, and none of us knew what to do next. Dad brought my banjo and a couple of books from Paul the Beatnik.

After my folks went home, I had another visitor. One of the priests from our parish came to see me. The priest and I knew each other. He had been there when my mom asked and then begged for a priest to visit my sick grandmother who lived just steps away from the church. He had been there when I implored the priests for help to deal with bullies. I wanted to turn the other cheek, but they would not stop coming after me. The good fathers were too busy to help but were quick to scold me when I ended up putting a bully in the hospital.

My grandfather had also punched the monsignor of our parish square in the nose several years prior. So, I wasn't expecting a lot when the priest walked into the room.

He mumbled a lot, so it was hard to understand everything he said, but one thing came out loud and clear. This affliction was a punishment from God.

I did not know what to say. I told myself that I misunderstood the priest, but then the curtain separating the two beds in the room flew open. A very large man with heavily tattooed arms started verbally tearing the good father a new one. Along with the insults, my roommate said that I was just a kid and that I did not, could not, do nothing to deserve what I was going through. He suggested that the priest leave before he got his ass kicked up between his shoulder blades.

The priest did the smart thing and left. I sat in stunned silence. My roommate threw me a copy of Hustler, saying, "This will take your mind off that shit."

He lit a cigarette and tossed me the pack. I told him I had been dying for a smoke since I woke up here. I fished a book of matches from the ashtray the hospital so thoughtfully provided. I paused before I struck the match.

"Girlie mags and cigarettes? Are you trying to get God to hit me with another seizure?"

He laughed out loud. "If it worked that way, I would have been struck down a long time ago."

We talked for a while. He kept telling me that I was just a kid. That God loved me. I was not being punished. I wanted to believe him, but I was so scared I thought I was going to cry.

My roommate tossed a copy of Penthouse at me, hitting me on the head.

"Have you got a library over there?" I asked him.

"A man has got to stay entertained," he said, moving slightly.

A catheter tube slid from under his blankets.

"What are you in for?" I asked him.

"Kidney stones, man." "I thought I had been hurt before, but this was the worst."

"Wait a second; you are reading girlie magazines with a catheter up your wazoo?"

We both started laughing. A nurse walked in, saw me smoking and reading dirty magazines, and just about went apeshit.

That only made us laugh harder. The two of us laughed until our sides hurt, and tears were in our eyes.

When I first saw my roommate, his tattoos were so exotic (it was a different time), and he was so big that I did not know what to expect. His kindness made the worst day of my life a happy memory. We laughed until we fell asleep.

The next day I had a bunch of tests and X-rays in the morning. I hate being poked and prodded, and by the time I got back to my room, I was feeling sorry for myself all over again. My roommate wasn't having any of it. He finally told me to take a walk.

"Where am I supposed to go?"

"Your dad brought your banjo. Go and play. Maybe music is what you need. Maybe he is trying to tell you something."

I felt ridiculous, but I grabbed my banjo with one hand, my IV stand with the other and stepped out into the hallway on my way to the sunroom. I got a few steps when someone from the next room called out to me. "Hey, is that a banjo?" Feeling as self-conscious as only a teenager in a hospital gown with a banjo can be, I mustered up my courage and walked in to visit with the patient.

I wasn't very experienced, but I knew even then that most folks expect the banjo player to walk in with a big smile. So that's what I did. I walked in, went right to his bedside and introduced myself. We talked for a bit and sang *Red River Valley,* and *You Are My Sunshine*. Then I plunked through *Wildwood Flower*. We said our goodbyes and I walked back into the hallway on my way to the sunroom. From the next room, a lady said. "Are you going to visit me? I love a banjo!"

I never did get to the sunroom. I spent the rest of that afternoon visiting my fellow patients. I saw people in pain; I saw people who were afraid. Sometimes I played for them, and sometimes we just sat together and prayed. As I went from room to room, I shook that self-aware feeling of foolishness because the people I was visiting were genuinely happy to see me. Somebody had cared enough to show up. Somebody showed up with a banjo and a smile and some old folk songs to sing of better days past and better days to come. Despite my hearing. Despite this new epilepsy thing, I was not handicapped. I was not useless. With each person I visited, with each patient or family member who thanked me, I realized that this was something special. By the time I got back to my room, I knew what I was going to do with my life. I propped my banjo up on the chair next to my bed. I sat on the edge of the bed and tried to process everything that had happened.

"How was the sunroom?" my roommate asked.

"Life-changing," I replied.

He laughed and tossed me a pack of smokes. I took one and tossed the rest back. I racked my brain for the next step. Do I take lessons to become a better musician? Would the banjo be enough, or should I learn other instruments? Where would I learn how to bring people together with music?

I had a simple idea, but it seemed like I had millions of questions that needed answers before I even started. Feeling restless, I picked up the books our beatnik friend had sent me. One caught my eye: *The Tao of Pooh*.

Tao? I remembered reading *The Tao Te Ching* a few years before. The opening verse read:

> *The way you go*
> *is not the way to go.*

The name you say
Is not its true name.

The book was cute but shoehorning Chinese philosophy into a storybook about a bear is the sort of clever literary stunt Lao Tzu was trying to avoid. I would leave the Pooh and take the Tao. I would follow the Tao to wherever I was supposed to go. I would take my banjo. The rest I would figure out along the way.

My roommate went home the next day. He left me well supplied with nudie magazines and cigarettes, but a nurse came in and threw them out as soon as he was gone.

I was in the hospital for almost a week. When I got back to school, some of my teachers made things tough — going as far as asking me to share with the class how it felt to be handicapped. It hurt, but they could all go to hell. School did not have much to teach me anyway.

I started cutting school, sometimes a class and sometimes the entire day, so I could head out into the city or the suburbs and wander wherever the Tao would take me. I found teachers. I gave impromptu lessons. I sang for and with the young and the old. The rich and the poor. Anybody who would listen.

What had seemed like the end of my world turned out to be the beginning of a new way of life. At first, my folks were less than thrilled to find that I was educating myself on the streets of Philadelphia, but after a while, I was able to convince my father to come along with me. Once he saw how happy I was, he started going out wandering with me. We have been making music together ever since. I guess I found my Way.

Fine Irish Lads

The rain fell from the pitch-black night sky in a great deluge. The cold was breathtaking, but I gritted my teeth and continued playing my banjo and waving at passing cars.

I tried to light a cigarette, but it quickly got drenched. To keep my mind off the chill, I experimented with matching the rhythm of my banjo to the patterns of the raindrops dancing across the blacktop highway. I was trying to catch a ride to a bar a few miles down the road. I was supposed to meet up with a band to play what would be my first ever paid gig.

I had met up with the leader of the band earlier that day. I was skipping school and hanging out in a run-down music store. This place was a real dump, but I had convinced myself that putting myself in places frequented by musicians would better my chances of the Tao leading me to a new teacher or adventure.

The shop was managed by my pal Lefty.

How do I describe Lefty? Skinny and tall. Stringy hair and greasy beard. Always wearing a leather biker jacket to hide the Barretta he carried. My mother laid eyes on him just once, and it was enough to make her fall to her knees and pray to Almighty God that I would stay away from him.

When I met Lefty, he had just bought a nice banjo from a trash collector. He got a lot of high-end instruments that way. The formula was simple:

1. Musician screws around.

2. Girlfriend finds out.

3. Girlfriend retaliates by tossing instruments worth thousands of dollars in the trash.

4. Trash collector sells the instruments to Lefty for a fraction of their value.

Lefty was looking for a teacher. I was looking for a place to hang out. We struck a deal. I would help him with the banjo and Lefty would help me with the guitar.

Lefty sweetened the deal by saying I could swipe a set of strings whenever I needed or wanted.

The shop was a pigsty full of cardboard electric guitars from Japan that nobody wanted, a shattered toilet where a guy who quit a heavy metal band weeks before they hit it big went into an existential crisis and a basement where the reprobates smoked weed in such quantity that you could smell it on the street.

Police raided the place so often that it stopped being surprising. I usually ended up getting bounced off the wall or slapped around for cracking wise at the officers.

I had no interest in the drug culture that usually gets associated with music. I had a hard enough time dealing with my hearing loss and epilepsy. I was not about to toss a drug-fueled cherry on top of that crap sundae. I navigated the debauchery by focusing on my music.

I was sitting on a broken amp playing my banjo when the band leader came into the shop to rent a sound system for the night.

He heard me playing and offered me my first job as a musician on the spot.

He spoke with a thick Irish brogue that, combined with my hearing, made it almost impossible for me to understand a word he was saying.

From what I could piece together, I was supposed to go to the bar, sit out the first set, and wait for the accordion player to get passed-out drunk. That would be my signal to step in and take his place playing Irish tunes on my banjo. For this night of adventure and music, I would make fifty bucks.

Fifty bucks was a king's ransom to me in those days.

There were a few problems with this wonderful plan. I knew nothing about Irish music, and I wasn't even old enough to drive. I decided that neither of these problems mattered. The Tao had led me to this adventure. I had to be brave and keep moving forward. Lefty stood behind the counter, shook his head, and said something that was sort of a mantra for him whenever something unusual would happen to me in the store.

"Pat, you know that this isn't normal, right? Weird shit like this never happens to normal people."

"It does when you follow the Tao."

So now I was soaking wet, chilled to the bone and flat broke by the side of the road. My teeth were chattering, and I was starting to wonder if I had made a mistake going out this late. Then a car stopped in the middle of the road.

The driver's side door opened. This shadow figure jumped out, yelling, "Get in. Get in!"

We were blocking traffic, so I didn't hesitate. I jumped into the passenger seat. We were rolling before I could buckle my seat belt.

The driver was perfect. Perfect hair, perfect face, perfect teeth, perfect muscles, and perfect clothes. He pointed to my banjo case and asked me, "That's a banjo, right?"

I tensed up a bit. Months earlier I hitched a ride, and the driver started talking about the movie Deliverance where Ned Beatty gets molested by hillbillies on a canoe trip. I jumped out of his car banjo and all, and as I hit the pavement, I heard the guy yell, "I was only joking!"

So, when this guy started asking about my banjo, I got nervous.

God damn you, Ned Beatty!

"Yes," I said, "it's a banjo."

The driver yelled, "Thank you, Jesus! Praise God! Thank you, God!"

He drummed his fists against the steering wheel in excitement.

I casually reached into my jacket pocket for the roll of nickels I kept handy. As the driver was praising God, I was getting ready to pop him in the jaw and bounce out of the car. He must have seen the expression on my face because he stopped hollering. He calmed down and told me his story.

He had been working as a male stripper, but then he found Jesus and got saved. He quit stripping and was now going to school to become a Pentecostal preacher. When he left home, his dad gave him a five-string banjo. Tonight, he had been driving around with his banjo on the back seat of his car praying for God to send him a banjo teacher. I looked over my shoulder, and there was indeed a banjo case on the back seat.

I believed him without hesitation. His story was just too bizarre to be anything but true. To top it off, he looked like a male stripper. Weeks later, he stopped by my house, and my very ladylike mother pulled me aside and said, "Oh Patrick, he is *gorgeous*!"

So, I offered to teach him to play the banjo. Right away, he asked if I could teach him to play like Earl Scruggs. I explained that I play and teach the old-time frailing style of banjo-like Grandpa Jones played. He looked a bit disappointed until I told him that, in my experience, frailing was easier to learn. I could teach him everything he needed to get started tonight before I met up with the Irish band.

He agreed but insisted on feeding me dinner.

A ride and a free meal? The Tao was taking good care of me. I was confident that nothing could go wrong.

I gave the stripper/preacher his banjo lesson. Sometimes I share the basics of frailing banjo with someone, and it just clicks. They get it, and I feel like a genius. That is not how this lesson went. Admittedly, frailing is a counterintuitive approach to making music with the five-string banjo. The right hand is held in a loose fist. You strike down on the strings with your middle fingernail and pluck the fifth string with your thumb.

I love this technique because perfection is nearly impossible. To freely make music with this down picking motion you need to be open to the idea of happy accidents. To say, "the hell with it" and dive into the song not caring about what could go wrong like a kid heading out in the dark of night to play in a bar and hitching a ride from a stripper/preacher.

I spent over an hour going over the basics with my new friend, but it was too abstract for him. When it was time for me to head out, I told him that I would arrange for my dad to give him a lesson, but we would have to come up with a cover story to explain how we met.

His jaw dropped. "Your dad doesn't know where you are?"

It had taken a few hours, but the soon to be preacher just realized that I was way too young to be hitching rides or playing in bars. He wanted to call my mom. He wanted to pray over me. I carefully and truthfully explained that I had no interest in drinking and that I was a student of Kenpo Karate and an instructor of Modern Arnis - a style of stick and knife fighting from the Philippines. I could take care of myself. I was just going to make music. What's the worst that could possibly happen?

He wasn't too happy about it, but he knew exactly where this so-called Irish bar was. We were soon parked close to the front door.

I shook his hand, and he prayed over me. I hopped out and waved as he drove away.

I walked into the bar and instantly had to resist the urge to turn around and walk home in the rain.

At first glance, it looked okay with very Irish tourist trap decor. What threw me for a loop was the clientele. The place was full of big, filthy, and mean-looking dudes. These were hard men and completely out of place with the Quiet Man decorations. As I stepped through the door, the whole place went silent. Every pair of eyes were fixed on me. I held up my banjo case and said, "I'm with the band tonight."

No reaction. Not even a smile. I slowly walked to the bar and parked myself on a stool with my banjo case between my knees. The bartender was a slip of a man. He pretended not to see me.

I sat on my barstool and waited for the band to arrive.

"You're an hour early."

I turned around, and the bartender was frowning at me. I looked at him quizzically.

"You're early. The band won't be here for an hour. Go away."

I laughed. "My dad is Irish Catholic. When I was growing up, he was always early. If we weren't an hour early, we were late."

He remained stone-faced.

"It's raining outside. Could I just have a Coke and wait for the band?"

"Is that all you want? A Coke?"

"I don't drink."

He silently poured me a Coke. I offered my hand in friendship, and he shook it with an iron grip.

"I'm Patrick," I said.

He almost smiled. "I'm Pat."

I reached in my pocket to pay for my drink, but Pat told me my soda was free.

I was happily sipping my drink when I felt bodies press close behind me. Rough hands spun me around on my bar stool. Three very large men had me cornered against the bar. I looked around for help, but everybody seemed to be dispassionately watching events unfold.

"So, we have a musician visiting us," one of the big dudes crowed. He opened his arms expansively. "What do you play, sir?"

It was hard to understand him. Partly because of his thick Irish brogue, partly because I was almost deaf at this point in my life. I was used to getting by through lip reading, body language, and old-fashioned intuition. Now I was faced with an alien culture, and I was lost.

Another tough guy said, "If he's a banjo player, he better prove himself."

I told them I would be happy to play for everybody. Just back up so I can open my banjo case.

Moments later, I was playing "Whiskey in the Jar," and people were enjoying it. I played the handful of Irish songs I knew amid nods of approval from all over the room. Then the three big dudes pressed in on me again. I sat helpless with my banjo on my lap. The biggest guy, standing right in front of me, leans in and says, "That's a nice banjo lad. Do you think I could play it with me dick?"

It takes a lot to leave me flabbergasted.

I was flabbergasted.

I asked him to repeat himself. The question was the same. "Do you think I could play your banjo with me dick?"

They had me cornered, but I wasn't going to back down. I puffed out my chest and said, "I'd like to see you try".

In a heartbeat, his red shorts were down by his ankles. As I sat there with my banjo in my lap, the big guy took hold of himself and began flogging his penis up and down the steel strings of my banjo.

It looked painful, and it wasn't very loud. Pat the bartender leaned over the bar, looked over my shoulder, saw the very drunk penis flopping up and down my banjo strings, and said, "Ah, he's at it again!"

Every person in the bar was watching for my reaction to this violation of my beloved musical instrument.

I thought about throwing a punch, but I had a feeling that this was a test or initiation of sorts. I looked around the room and said, "So that's how they play the banjo back home in Ireland."

The big guy stopped molesting my banjo, pulled up his pants, and looked at me quizzically.

"You're Irish?"

"My banjo-dicking friend, I'm so Irish my great aunt Kate died with her lips on the Blarney Stone!"

They all shouted and raised a pint to poor aunt Kate.

Somebody tried to hand me a beer, but Pat quietly exchanged it for a coke.

Pat grabbed my shirt and pulled me close. "You're welcome here. No drinking and no fucking around."

He didn't have to tell me twice. "Yes, sir. Thank you, sir." I said. Pat nodded in approval and went back to pulling pints for the regulars.

One of the banjo molesters came back around and asked about Aunt Kate. I told him as much of the story as I knew.

"They lowered her down to kiss the Blarney Stone. When they pulled her up, she was stone dead."

Banjo-dicker asked me if the whole family was Irish.

"My dad is one hundred percent Irish. My mon is half Irish and half Pennsylvania Dutch. My grandfather is always telling me terrible Irish jokes."

"Like what?"

"Did you know that you can't hang an Irishman with a wooden leg?"

"Is that so?"

"You have to use a rope."

The guy laughed a little too hard at that one.

Just before the band arrived, I managed to slip into the men's room to wipe my banjo down with wet paper towels and regret some of my life choices up to that point.

I came out of the men's room and saw Pat giving the bandleader a rundown of what had happened, complete with a pantomime of my banjo being molested.

They both pointed at me and laughed.

Then the bandleader told the group, and as he introduced me to everyone, they all had a wiseass remark to make about my banjo possibly getting pregnant. I took it all pretty well if I do say so myself.

The band was much larger than I expected. Two vocalists, a guy playing tin whistle, bodhran, accordion, rhythm guitar, and bass. I decided not to mention my hearing problems. I would try to get by as best I could, and if I couldn't do the job, I wouldn't take the money. As instructed, I sat out most of the first set.

Almost all the songs were about the bloody, bloody British. Some were about the Black and Tans. I quickly realized that this was not just Irish folk music. These were all IRA songs.

"Patrick," I asked myself, "what have you gotten yourself into now?"

In addition to the IRA centric songs, another alarming thing was the sheer amount of alcohol these men and women were consuming. I had never seen anything like this before.

After a while, the accordion player started to make mistakes. Then he started playing different tunes from what the band was playing. That was my signal to step up to a mic.

The first couple of songs I played with the band were rough, but I quickly relaxed, and the music seemed to take over. I had never heard most of these songs before, but everything just clicked.

As the night progressed, the men and women in the audience started separating. The girls all danced with each other while the men got plastered. We started mixing in pretty melodies with the rebel songs.

Three AM came in the blink of an eye. I had school later in the morning and I had to get home and back into the house somehow. I helped the band break down the sound system and dawdled around hoping to get paid, but the bandleader had other plans. He said, "We don't get paid until the next gig."

"This was a one-night job for me."

"Not anymore, you're one of us now."

Pat the bartender poured me a Coke and Annie, who owned the place, served me an awesome roast beef sandwich. I walked home in that early morning darkness singing one of the songs I had learned that night.

She is handsome, she is pretty
She is the belle of Belfast city
She is a-courting one, two, three
Pray, can you tell me who is she?

The Tao had led me safely through a wild night of adventure. I was part of a band!

The tricky part would be, how long could I keep sneaking out of the house before I got caught?

To top it off, I had school in a few hours.

Riding The Rails

The desire to play my Dobro 33H guitar burned in my teenage brain like a fever. The problem was that I could find no remedy for my affliction. I bought books that were mostly pictures of sad old men and pages of tablature that looked like Phoenician hen scratches. I tried to find a teacher, but acoustic country blues guitar is a highly specialized skill. The one instructor I found wanted fifty bucks a lesson. I told him I wouldn't pay that much for Jesus Christ to give me unicycle lessons. The situation seemed hopeless. The harder I tried it seemed the problem pushed back with equal force.

Then it hit me to stop trying. I don't mean give up. I am no quitter. I decided to stop searching and instead start putting myself in places where a teacher could find me.

My first choice was Philadelphia subway platforms. I could walk from My home in Havertown, PA, to the 69th street terminal and ride the subway trains all through Philly.

I started on weekends, but quickly realized that my chances would be better during the week – and that meant skipping school. I knew there would be hell to pay, but I had to find a teacher! My plan was so simple; it had to work. I would find a busy platform, pull my Dobro 33-H guitar out of its case, and start playing as best I could. I only left my case open for tips if I really needed the money. Busking brought too much heat from the police and predators. Sometimes people would hear my music and smile and sometimes I got beat up. Philadelphia was a tough town in the 1980s. I met some nice people, but weeks went by with no sign of a teacher. I began to lose hope. I continued going into the city even after it seemed silly with so many wasted days spent wandering the city toting a heavy guitar case.

It happened after I had stopped trying. I was out busking – no longer searching. There were a few dollars and some change in my guitar case. The day was going so well that I even had a pack of Marlboros and a lighter in the case pocket. I was half-heartedly strumming Sportin' Life Blues and trying to work my way through Stagolee.

"What in the *hell* do you think you're doing? You don't call that the blues? My God, boy. Give me that guitar before you hurt somebody."

He snatched my beloved guitar from my hands, fished the cigarettes out of the case pocket and lit up one of my Marlboros while he touched up the tuning.

"Hey, who are you?" I asked, and then shouted, "Give me back my guitar!"

"I ain't gonna hurt your guitar, boy," he said. "And it's not like a nice white boy from the suburbs can't afford a new guitar. If you shut up, you might learn something. I'm gonna show you something now, son. Think of it as a public service because I can't let you go on like that. Hurt people's ears playing like that."

Then he started to play.

I knew my Dobro was special, but until that moment, I did not know *how* special. His rough hands took hold of the strings, and my guitar sang, wailed and screamed. The rhythm seemed to fill the subway platform like a wind. The bass strings boogied, and the high strings rang out. The people waiting for the next train started to react to the music. I had known intellectually that the blues could make people move their bodies and now I was seeing it happen. Guys in business suits bopped their heads and tapped their feet. People clapped along to the rhythm and a guy wearing a rain poncho on a sunny day danced beautifully. I saw almost everything I wanted out of the guitar happen at that moment. He stopped playing with a flourish.

"Now, that ain't nothing. Nothing! Put a guitar like this in the right hands and then you'd have something. I can pick a little blues, but you. . . I don't know what the hell you were doing."

"That's what my dad says. He comes out when I practice and says, that ain't the blues. That's shit and goes back inside."

"Your daddy is a smart man."

He handed the guitar back to me.

"Make me an E chord."

I made an E chord. He reached over, lifted my fingers off the fretboard and changed the way I made the chord. My left middle finger now fretted the fourth and fifth strings at the second fret. I was able to fret two bass strings with one finger by placing my fingertip between the strings. My finger caught just enough of the two strings to work. My left index finger was on the third string at the first fret. I was making the E chord with two fingers! I strummed the chord. It sounded terrible.

"I can't fret two strings at once!" I yelled.

He yelled right back, 'Yes, you can! Practice!"

I fought with the E chord until it almost sounded good. Now it was time to add the right hand to the equation.

We counted out a rhythm in 4/4 time. "One, two, three, four." On the first and third beat, I plucked the sixth string with my thumb. On the second and fourth beat I strummed down across the strings to sound the E chord. Counting out loud, "one, two, three, four" over and over again. He took the guitar back and played the thumb-brush rhythm while holding the E chord.

"With a little practice, you can do this."

He did. . . Something, and suddenly he was playing the shuffle rhythm again. Time seemed to stop. The noise of the subway station, already faint because of my bad hearing, seemed to fade until there was nothing in the world but me, my new friend and my guitar. There was so much I wanted to ask him. I did not even know his name!

Sadly, I knew that time was short. I had to take in whatever he was willing to share with me. I had put myself where a teacher could find me. Now the lesson was happening. A quiet voice deep inside me said to soak in every part of this moment because it may never happen again.

He shared with me how to create the shuffle rhythm. It seemed simple enough in concept, but it would take years of effort to even begin making it roll smoothly from my guitar. Start with that God-cursed two-finger E chord and add the thumb-brush rhythm pattern. Now add some bounce. After plucking the sixth string with the thumb, pick the second string with the right index finger. As the right thumb strums down, hammer your left ring finger on the second string at the second fret. Pick the open first string with the right index finger as the left-hand releases the E chord. As you begin to repeat the pattern, hammer your two-finger E chord as you pluck the sixth string.

We went over that a couple of times. It sounded so good when he did it. I was terrible – and he got a good laugh at my expense. He said I would get it if I practiced. Then he taught me how to make an A chord by bending my middle finger to fret the second, third, and fourth strings at the second fret. This one-finger barre chord would allow me to roll the A chord by alternating between my index finger on the first fret and my middle finger on the second. This trick also works for the B chord at the fourth fret if you compensate for the first string. This all seemed simplistic broken down but played at speed; the rhythm made my heart beat faster. It still does more than thirty years later!

I asked a few questions knowing I would get home and think of a million I should have asked. He cracked jokes and stressed the rhythm. He got up to leave. He pocketed my Marlboros and scooped the money from my guitar case. I said I did not know how to thank him. He said the money and the cigarettes would do just fine. Then he got on the subway car and disappeared from my life as quickly as he had arrived. I never saw him again. To this day, I do not know his name. He never gave me a name for the guitar pattern he taught me, so I started calling it the Subway Shuffle. Twenty years later I shared the Subway Shuffle on the then-new web platform YouTube. Thousands of aspiring guitar players picked up the rhythm in much the same manner as it was taught to me. It was scary and frustrating going out into the city over and over again hoping to cross paths with a teacher. After the Subway Shuffle I went back to that platform many times, but I never saw him again. I did meet other teachers who introduced me to even more music. If I had stayed home none of this would have happened. If I had played it safe taking regular lessons, I never would have found the music that was right for me.

After that day, I began looking at everyone I met as a potential teacher. Not just for music. As the years progress, I try to remain open to the lessons those teachers have to share – even when the lesson is hard to hear.

There is an old pop-culture saying, incorrectly attributed to the Buddha that goes something like "when the student is ready, the master will appear." In my experience, a better way to put that would be "if you put yourself out there, a teacher will eventually find you." The hard part is going out day after day, long past the point where a rational person would quit – and then going out again. I would give anything to see my guitar friend again, but God or fate or the Tao decreed that we would meet just once. My teenage years are long past me. I am past grown up and heading to growing old, but if I saw his face again, I would run to him like a child. Eager to tell him everything that has happened since that long-ago afternoon when he made country blues guitar accessible to me. His moment of kindness coming from or going to someplace on the Market-Frankford Line opened a world of music for me and my students.

God bless that mysterious guitar man!

I've Looked at Clowns From Both Sides Now

When I was a little boy, I dreamed about joining the circus. I wanted to be a clown. It looked like a great job, performing under the big top and making people laugh.

My parents tried to steer me towards a more practical trade. Dad bought me a kid's carpentry set with a hammer to drive wooden pegs into boards. I got my finger stuck in one of the peg holes, and everybody on our block got involved in trying to get my finger free. My father wound up using a hacksaw to cut me loose. To this day, it is on the short list of childhood moments that still make my dad upset.

Never ask my dad about:

- Cutting my finger free from the carpentry playset.
- The trip where I slathered the entire interior of a Gremlin with melted bubble gum.
- The day I got my head stuck in an iron railing.

There are others, but those are the top three.

As the years went by my desire to be a clown did not waver. I read books on the history of the circus, carnivals, and sideshows. I never did learn how to juggle, and I never got my hands on a unicycle.

My grandfather took me to see an old-fashioned circus. The clowns called for a volunteer. I was too shy to raise my hand, so grandpop pinched me. Hard. I jumped up with a yell, and the clowns carried me off. I was under the big top. With clowns. It was my first time in front of a big crowd, but I really had a good time. The clowns dressed me up in a girdle and bra. Then things got weird. I looked up at my grandfather up in the bleachers, and he was laughing so hard that his false teeth fell out in his lap! After that, I was even more determined. I didn't need school. I was going to find a way to join a circus – maybe without the cross-dressing.

I just about drove my parents nuts. Circus, circus, circus. Blah, blah, blah. My dad tried to tell me that there was more to the job than fun and games, but I would not listen. So, dad took me to see the next circus that came through town. This was a much bigger affair, and I was in heaven. All through the show, I was saying that this was how I wanted to spend my life. Dad just nodded. Never said a word.

After the show, dad says, "Let's take a walk."

We went all the way around the big top, and that's when we saw it.

Clowns. Just not as I was used to seeing them.

The clowns had dragged the canvas floor out from the big top and were now out in the hot sun scraping and sweeping all the shit dropped by elephants, camels, horses, zebras, lions, tigers, and God only knows what else. Some of the clowns were bare-chested. All of them were sweating profusely. All of them beshitted to some degree.

A stout man with clown white running from his face into his chest hair spotted us. He puffed on his cigar and waved at me. "Hello, little boy, welcome to the circus!"

I grabbed my father's hand and whispered that, maybe, we should get to the car. After all, mom was waiting for us.

As we were heading home, dad asked me if I still wanted to join the circus. I said no.

Every profession has two sides. The public sees the glamour of the big top, but they don't see what happens after – and it's always shoveling shit, one way or another.

When dad took me to see *The Blues Brothers* a few years later, I experienced the same inspiration and reality. The movie showed the exciting side of music, but it also portrayed, in cartoon foolishness, the downside of making music for a living. Difficulty finding work, getting paid, getting stared at in nice restaurants (even in my best outfit a swanky place goes quiet when I walk in) and stuff like that. They even showed the personal dilemmas that come with the job in the scene where Matt Guitar Murphy runs off with the band despite his wife's pleas to stay home.

Halfway through *The Blues Brothers,* I tugged on my dad's sleeve, pointed at the screen and said, "That's what I'm gonna do, dad!"

Dad laughed just like he had when I talked of clowns, but he did not know then that music has manure piles that I was not afraid to shovel.

Harmonica Joe

"Hey kid, do you want to make a couple of dollars?"

I was not so naïve as to be unaware of the usual course of action a kid was supposed to take when an old man in a raincoat asks a question like that. Even so, this guy looked harmless, and I was more than curious about the huge chromatic harmonica he had pulled from his pocket, so I didn't run like hell.

He spoke with a cadence all his own and an accent I could not place. He waved his harmonica like a wand as he spoke.

"You break out that guitar, and we can make a few bucks. Maybe get some lunch. Maybe enough to get some burgers to take home with me. I have a hot plate, and they heat up good. Come on, kid. Play a tune with Harmonica Joe."

I was here because my mother wanted somebody to keep an eye on my grandfather. At this moment grandpop was trolling the slot machine pits in one of the casinos. He wasn't interested in gambling. Oh, he might toss a few bucks into the slots, but all he had in mind was chatting up the little old lady bingo queens.

He found a service outside of town that would take us to Atlantic City. The ticket cost ten dollars, but once you got to the casino, you would get ten dollars in quarters to prime the spending pump. My grandfather got to gamble and bird-dog by the ocean for free – and he loved free stuff. I only came along because mom thought that somebody should watch out for him.

I had just gotten my Dobro 33H guitar, and I took it with me everywhere. It was so big and heavy that carrying it onto the bus was a real hassle, but I said to myself, "you never know who you might meet," and I dragged the case with me. The last time I had taken this trip with grandpop I managed to play some slots by telling security I was with the band.

If I happened to hit a small jackpot grandpop would swipe my quarters, saying, "You shouldn't gamble." Sigh.

On this trip, I didn't get past the door. A security guard spotted me and escorted me out. "But I'm with the band!" I protested. The guard didn't even smile. Grandpop left me. He shouted, "serves you right for being a wiseass!" and went in to play and chase ladies. I was on my own. On the boardwalk. On a cool day. Without a dime in my pocket. Grandpop had even kept my free roll of quarters from the tour bus!

I wandered around aimlessly until I saw an old man covered with seagulls.

He was trying to eat a hot dog in this arthritic kind of slouch over a trash can. He looked like his back was too messed up to stand upright. Pigeons and seagulls were lined up on his back and shoulders trying to reach around his head and snatch his hot dog. There were so many birds piled on top of him that I could not see his face. I moved closer to get a better look. He noticed me and raised his head to look me in the eye – or tried to. A seagull hopped on his head and knocked his hat down over his eyes.

"Hey old timer, that's a good trick with all of those birds."

"Help me out, kid. Get these damn birds off of me!"

I cracked up and went to work swatting the gulls and pigeons away so that he could finish his hot dog. It hit me that the hot dog didn't look fresh.

"Thank you for the help.

"Hell of a thing when a man can't eat his lunch in peace," I extended my hand. "I'm Patrick"

"Yes, you are. I'm Joe"

We shook hands.

"Patrick, did I tell you that I used to be on the radio?" He Pulled a large chromatic harmonica from his coat pocket and played a jazz riff. "Say hello, and what do you know? It's Harmonica Joe on the radio!"

He pronounced radio as, "ra-di-oh." He pointed at my guitar case. "You Play?"

"A little. I'm not very good yet."

Then, waving his shiny chromatic harp like a wizard casting a spell, Harmonica Joe asked me if I wanted to make a couple of dollars.

I said yes, of course.

Right away, Joe started talking a mile-a-minute. Waving his harp with one hand and the last bites of his seagull and pigeon pecked hot dog in the other. "The first thing we have to do is find ourselves a spot. You've got to have a good spot. In front of casinos is no good because everybody going in or out is either broke or saving up to go broke. You know the house always wins? Don't gamble, son. It'll ruin you as quick as a showgirl. I should know. Now the spot. We want a spot where we can hit the couples. Couples are good because you sing to the girl and the guy has to give you a tip, or he'll look like a heel."

"So, we sing to the girl and find a good spot."

"That's right! You're getting the idea. I might get myself some lunch today! I told you my name was Harmonica Joe? I used to be on the radio!" He played his riff and sang, "Say hello and what do you know? It's Harmonica Joe on the radio!"

We wandered until we found a spot he liked. We were close to a couple of tourist trap shops with cheesy tee shirts and salt water taffy on display.

"Get out your guitar. Leave your case open – casually – so people have a place to leave a tip. I'll call the songs. Do you know any jazz numbers?"

"No"

"Good. That's what we'll play."

I must have looked nervous because Joe gave me a pep talk.

"You get to a chord you don't know, just move your hands up and down like you are strumming, but don't make any sound. Just smile at the people and move. Out here by the ocean, they can't hear most of what we are playing, so just do your best and smile. When they can't hear you, they'll assume that the ocean is drowning you out."

He went over more things and more or less taught me all about the art of busking. He taught me to casually draw attention to my guitar case so that people would remember to leave a tip.

There was more – a lot more. It was cool because Joe had this down to a science. We worked the people passing by as easy as you please while we played and sang old songs. When a couple stopped to listen, Joe would fuss over the girl while I made contact with the boyfriend and kicked the guitar case. No way he wouldn't leave a tip after Joe took his girl by the hand for a few dance steps. When families stopped, Joe would entertain the kids while I signaled for dad to drop a few bucks our way. I never had to say a thing. Just "accidentally" bump my guitar case hard enough to rattle the change and maybe shoot the mark a look.

Oh my, did the money flow that day.

This whole time Harmonica Joe talked about performing. He talked about the places he had been, but mostly he talked about how the game works. He said that entertaining was not just about playing well, but also making the audience feel good about listening to you. I don't know how long we played that afternoon. Time flew by because I was having so much fun learning from Joe and watching him work the crowd.

It all came to a halt when Joe knocked my guitar case closed, kicked the case under a bench, and stashed the harp in his coat pocket. Then Joe just stood there like he was asking me the time. I couldn't figure out what was happening until the cop walked over.

"Nice try, Joe, but I have been watching you two for a while now."

"Why hello, officer. Lovely day isn't it?"

"Joe, how many times have I told you that I don't want you panhandling out on my boardwalk?"

"Panhandling? You're acting like every musician out on the street is some kind of bum!"

"Joe, you *are* a bum!"

Before Joe could say anything, the cop turned to me.

"Who are you?"

I gave him a big grin. "It's okay; I'm with the band."

He didn't seem to think that was any funnier than the security guard who threw me out of the casino.

"So, you're out here learning to be a bum?"

"I thought I'd give it a try. If it didn't work out, I could always be a co. . ."

Joe cut me off before I could deliver the punch line. "He's just a kid playing a little bit of guitar with old Joe. Nothing wrong with that is there, officer?"

The cop gave me the hairy eyeball.

I grinned back at him.

He finally relaxed and started to laugh. "Well, you guys didn't sound too bad. Matter of fact, you sound better than the guys further down the boardwalk, but they ain't breaking the law because they have a license."

I started to say something, but Joe kicked me hard. Then he gave me the signal to keep my mouth shut.

The cop looked us over again, gave a deep sigh, shook his head, and said, "I'm going to take a walk. When I come back, I want both of you gone. I'm sick of telling you this, Joe. I don't want to see you again today."

So that was that. Time to hit the bricks. I was sad that it was over, but I had a great time and Joe had taught me so much.

As I dragged my guitar case out from under the bench, it hit me that I was exhausted. This had been a lot of fun, but it was also a lot of work!

I flipped my case open, and I was shocked at the amount of money it contained. The marks had thrown in change and bills. A lot of fives and ones at first glance. Joe took a peek, and his face brightened up.

"Not a bad take for a little bit of work. Fifty-fifty sound good to you?"

I thought about it for a second and decided I could do better than that. I scooped up the money and handed it to Joe.

"Here. Take it and get yourself those burgers."

Joe tried to argue with me, but I wouldn't take any of the money for myself. I didn't need it. I had learned so much from Joe that this was nowhere near what he deserved.

He took the money, and we said our goodbyes. Joe gave me a quick hug and disappeared into the crowd.

Joe had just left. I was squaring away my guitar case when my grandfather came running yelling, "what the hell are you doing?" Grandpop had seen me handing over a fistful of cash to a man that my grandfather said, "looked like a bum." My grandfather went on to berate me. That Joe was going to use the money to get drunk and that I was a jackass for thinking otherwise.

"Grandpop, he was hungry. He needed the money to buy lunch and some extra to take home. All he wanted was a couple of cheeseburgers."

"If you believe that you must be stupid. Don't you know anything?"

We were walking past the McDonalds on the boardwalk, just killing time before the tour bus took us home. As we walked past the golden arches, the door opened and out stepped Joe with a cup of coffee and a bag of cheeseburgers. Joe saw me, and he waved his bag of burgers, shouting,

"God bless you, boy! I got my lunch, and I got some to take home! Goodbye, and don't forget old Harmonica Joe!"

I shouted back, "Say hello, and what do you know? It's Harmonica Joe on the radio!"

For the first time in my life, my grandfather didn't have anything to say.

In the years since I think about Joe. I wonder who he was. I wonder if other people took the time to see the man under the years and worn clothes.

The universe is vast. The stars we see at night went out ages ago, but the light is reaching us just now tonight. If you desire to learn art, music, mathematics, language, dance, or anything else, all you have to do is look around you. There are teachers everywhere. Every person you meet has something to teach you if you are open to the lesson.

Maybe Joe was a bum, but I am grateful I took the time to get to know him. To learn from him. He has been in my thoughts across America and Europe, and his lessons have gotten me out of more than one tight spot.

Thank you, Joe. God bless you.

The Old Man and the C Chord

"Coffee Time."

The melodic voice rang out from the speakers of my boom-box radio. He talked about his favorite coffee and how his woman made it just right, but she was gone. He had to find her. Then Mississippi John Hurt began to play his guitar, and I was never the same.

Every Sunday night the public radio station in Philadelphia ran a folk music show. A lot of what they broadcasted did not interest me, but every now and then they would play something cool and unexpected. I would sit with my good ear pressed against one of the speakers on my boom-box. If something awesome ended up on the playlist, I would record it and play the tape endlessly for the rest of the week.

When they played the recording of John Hurt singing *Coffee Blues* to a live audience, I completely freaked out. I had never heard a guitar that sounded so alive. Happy. Free.

The next day I set out on a journey to discover how to make my guitar ring out like Mississippi John Hurt. I talked to Lefty first. Word was that he had once been a good Chicago blues guitar player.

I figured blues is blues, but Lefty was quick to point out that his brand of music was all about electric guitar players. BB King, Albert King, Howling Wolf, Elmore James, Magic Sam, and so many other great musicians. The stuff that had hooked me by the gills was country blues guitar, and that was all acoustic. I had heard Mississippi John Hurt, but he was just one of dozens of acoustic guitar players from the deep south. Lefty went on.

"Nobody cares about country blues. There ain't no money in it, and no white boy from suburbia was going to figure it out on his own."

"I hear what you are saying, but I don't care about money. I don't want to perform. I just want my guitar to be that expressive."

Lefty shook his head.

"Old-time banjo and country blues guitar. You have a thing for shit nobody likes anymore."

"That is just because they don't hear it anymore. When I play, people will say, 'I want to do that!'"

Lefty just laughed and called me a lunatic.

After the dubious pep-talk from Lefty, I started looking for books on country blues guitar. The volumes were expensive and filled with photographs of old black men and their guitars. Most of them were artists I had never heard before. Every Sunday I would call the folk radio show and request one of the names from the photographs so I could hear them. Memphis Minnie, Charley Patton, Gus Cannon, Reverend Gary Davis, Blind Willie Johnson and more. Each request drew out an entirely new world of musical possibilities that left me breathless with joy. A voice, a guitar, and skill were the only ingredients, but each musician sounded unique. The blues seemed as vast and as deep as the ocean.

Inspired by the music, I dove right into the guitar tab included with the books. Tab, or tablature, is a way of writing out the mechanics of a guitar song. It tells you what strings to strike, fret, pluck, or strum. Most of us would assume that knowing the finger mechanics of a song is all it takes. Practice hard enough, and a monkey could do it. Right? Nope!

When I started trying to use tab for country blues guitar songs, my playing went to hell in a handbasket. Instead of making music, I was making disjointed guitar sounds. Noises.

I kept practicing, even though I knew that I was on the wrong path. I needed to keep working. I decided that I would work without thought of progress until the Tao brought a teacher to me. I had to be open to the lesson, even if It was something I did not want to hear.

It took almost a year.

I had started playing a three-finger roll where my thumb played a bass note followed by my middle finger picking a note, then my index finger and back to my middle finger. It gave me four quarter notes to a measure, but outside of *House of the Rising Sun,* it started to sound mechanical. I used the tab from my books to attempt John Hurt songs like *Stagolee* or *My Creole Belle*, but it always sounded like an angry monkey was throwing poo at the guitar strings. It was terrible.

A friend called and invited us to come to a barbecue and pickin' party. He owned a folk music shop, so we believed him when he said it was going to be a huge turnout.

I loaded my banjo in the truck, but I decided to leave my guitar at home for this trip. I wanted to focus on what I was good at and show off my hot frailing licks.

Dad called bullshit on that. He said the day I leave my guitar at home would be the day I need it most.

I loaded my guitar into the truck.

We drove about two hours to get to the pickin' party, and we were all alone. Even the crickets were quiet. We drove to the music shop, and everybody was running around in circles trying to get ready. We told them that the park was a ghost town and they told us that we must have been in the wrong place. We waited for a while and then headed to the park with the folks from the store. It turned out that we had been at the right place all along, and it was still empty. As the day progressed a few more people showed up, but nowhere enough for a monster jam session.

"In the case. . . is that a Dobro?" I turned around to see who was talking to me. He was a large man with very square features like a character drawn by Jack Kirby. He had a shock of snow-white hair on his head and the palest blue eyes I have ever seen. What really caught my attention was his hands. His fingertips were so calloused they looked like talons.

I was instantly curious. "Yes, a Dobro 33H."

The old man nodded and walked away. I tried to keep talking to him, but he was not interested. I wandered around talking to the handful of musicians in attendance.

My dad tried to get a jam started, but everybody was reluctant to start playing.

I wound up in a conversation with a very nervous man who brought a custom banjo he had built. The instrument was exquisite, and the resonator was a mosaic — a creation of marquetry, oil paint, stone, and gold. A Frank Frazetta inspired portrait of a naked lady with comically huge knockers riding a black panther. I just stood there in awe. It was a work of amazing craftsmanship and terrible taste.

A large hand fell on my shoulder — the white-haired man.

"Get away from the creepy guy with the titty banjo. Get your guitar and come with me."

A second chance with the calloused hand guy? "Yes! Thank you, sir."

We walked to the edge of the park and found a shady spot in some bushes, out of sight from the rest of the group.

"Ummm. . . I don't know if I should be following strange men into the woods."

He laughed. "You are correct, but today I want shade, and I don't want to put on a show."

He opened a fairly new guitar case and lifted out a Guild F-30 that looked like it had been through a woodchipper more than once. He quickly tuned his guitar. Then he started to play. I heard a bit of all the country blues musicians I loved. The bass notes bounced, the rhythm had a strut, and the melody just danced over everything.

"Get your Dobro out. Let's pick."

My heart jumped up into my throat. "I'm not very good yet."

He shot me a look.

I brought my Dobro out of its case and fumbled with my bulky chromatic tuner. I noticed that the old guy was frowning, so I told him everything. My hearing. Using my teeth to hear the guitar. Frustration with tab. All of it. He listened to my tale of woe. Then he asked me to play something. I tried to play *My Creole Belle*.

"What the fuck was that?"

"*My Creole Belle*."

"Jesus. I couldn't tell what you were trying to play. That was so bad it hurt my feelings."

I couldn't help but laugh, but I was still so frustrated. "I bought the books on playing blues, but all they give you is tab. None of it makes any sense."

My guitar case was open, and there was a stack of tab sheets I had photocopied or torn out of books. My new friend scooped them up and looked through them. "Oh, *those* books." Then he crumpled the pages into balls and threw them into the bushes.

"Hey!"

"Those were not helping you. Quite the opposite."

"But what else am I going to do?"

"First, take off the fingerpicks."

"What?"

"The alternating thumb is more from the influence of Merle Travis and Chet Atkins. I think that isolated alternating thumb makes everything sound like Polka music, not the blues."

I had to agree. "It does sometimes have a creepy sameness to it, but none of my friends hear it."

"Chet is one of the most powerful men in Nashville. If you want a career, you have to say he is the greatest."

"Then who is the greatest?"

"Some guy nobody ever heard of."

"Oh."

"Fame isn't about how good you are. It's about how good your agent or promoter convinces people you are."

"Like the Daffy Duck cartoon?"

"*Sleepy Lagoof*? I love that one too."

He started to play *My Creole Belle* again, but he started to sing *Richland Woman Blues*.

> *The red rooster says*
> *Cocka doodle do do*
> *The Richmond woman says*
> *Any dude will do*

I stared at him, open-mouthed in surprise.

He laughed and said that the melody came from a fiddle tune.

My mommy told me
If I be goody
She's gonna buy me
A rubber dolly

Once I was over the shock that my favorite Mississippi John Hurt song got its melody from a weird fiddle tune we went to work.

First, the right hand. His advice was to stay away from books and experts. Instead, do what my heroes did and use what I already knew. I could frail the banjo pretty well, so why not start there? At first, I thought he meant trying to use basic frailing on the guitar. He said not to be so damn literal.

"Try playing a bass note with your thumb, strumming down with your thumb and up-picking with your index finger."

"Oh! Just like frailing banjo!"

Then we turned our attention to the left hand. As I noted before, the fingers of his left hand were so calloused that they looked like talons. The fretboard of his Guild guitar was deeply worn. He must have noticed me staring.

"I go through a fretboard every two years or so. After my wife died, I started practicing all day, and I haven't stopped."

"I'm sorry."

He waved my words away. "Now let's look at chords."

We started with the key of D because he said it was a little easier. We took the standard D chord where the first string is fretted at the second fret, the second string at the third fret and the third string at the second fret. We started with the bass note, strum, and up-pick pattern and added a pinch on the first string at the same time as the bass note. The timing was the same, but the sound was radically different.

"Now, the fun part." He said.

On the pinch, while holding the D major chord, we reached out with our pinky to fret the first string at the fifth fret. After the pinch, release the first string at the fifth fret so that the strum sounded like a plain old D chord. We went over some more variations for the key of D, then we moved to the Key of C.

Again, we were holding the standard C, F, and G chord shapes, but we were changing the chord shapes to draw out melody notes. The changes were easy to keep track of because they were all part of the C major scale. My head was spinning, but I was elated. I could do this! This made sense!

"I don't know how to thank you."

He waved my words away. Again.

"Those books you were using. They were not written to help you. They were written to show you how smart the author is - or thinks he is. A lot of them play just as funky as the tab you were trying to use."

I spotted my dad wandering the picnic grounds, looking for me. I told my mysterious friend that I wanted to check on him.

"You are lucky." He said.

"Lucky? I'm using my teeth to hear my guitar!"

"Sure, but you can hear it that way. You also have your dad and that shiny Dobro. You are luckier than you can begin to imagine."

"I guess you are right."

As I put down my guitar to go check on dad, my friend told me he was going to leave. I tried to talk him into meeting my dad, but he was determined to go. We shook hands. He probably would have punched me if I tried to hug him. I told him my name. He said his, but his head was down so I could not read his lips and he did not react when I said that I didn't catch that. I packed up my guitar and rushed out to tell dad what had just happened. We looked in the parking lot, but he had already left.

I never ran into him again.

On the ride home, dad asked me about the Tao.

"The Tao is the rhythm of the universe, dad. Not what you want, but how things need to be."

"So, you just wait for a guitar guy and eventually one shows up?"

"Yes, but it's not just showing up like, 'Here I am!' it's showing up with what I need when I need it."

"And this is the third time?"

"Yeah. The first guy was the man on the subway platform. The second was the blues band in the music store."

"What's next?"

"I don't know. We go home, and I try to put the puzzle pieces together."

Dad nodded. After that, whenever I got frustrated dad would say, "Follow the Tao. Relax and follow the Tao."

It took years for me to put those puzzle pieces together. We tried to find the man with the calloused hands and the worn-out Guild to no avail. Even our friend who owned the music store that repaired his guitars refused to give us his contact information. "He is really reclusive. I don't know why he even came to the picnic that day."

Dad shot me a knowing look and mouthed silently, "The Tao."

I nodded.

We were supposed to meet that day and no more. If I pushed things and found the old man things would not go well. Still, there are nights when my guitar seems to tune itself, and the melodies to a million songs are just one finger or fret away from my C major chord, that I wish I could thank the old man with the Guild guitar. I learned so much during our conversation in that shady place between the park and the cornfield.

Amish Elvis

Amish Elvis towered over me, bellowing, "Is this your cheater, boy?"

Amish Elvis was talking to me?

Okay, what the hell is a cheater?

I racked my brain until Amish Elvis finally waved my expensive Shubb capo under my nose between his thumb and index finger. His lip curled in a moue of distaste—like a hypochondriac who just found a toenail clipping in his cornflakes.

I plastered a relived smile across my face. "Oh! My capo! Thank you, sir. I did not realize that I had dropped it."

I reached out to take my capo, but Amish Elvis closed his fingers around the gadget in a tight fist.

Crap. This was about to get weird.

We were back at the Lyons Park Fiddle Festival. The place where I had performed with my dad for the first time a few years ago. The crazy person holding my capo hostage was a guy I thought of as Amish Elvis.

Amish Elvis was a big guy. His imitation gold belt buckle was the size of my head. He wore immaculate white suits with music notes on the lapels, so you knew he was a musician even before he started singing or banging out a rhythm on his Martin dreadnaught guitar. Between his snazzy outfit and his Amish beard (sans mustache) I just thought of him as Amish Elvis.

The first time I saw Amish Elvis, he was playing a gospel medley with a pickup band, and they were good. As they began to play, *I Saw The Light* somebody from the audience rushed the stage and started flat-footing. Just dancing up a storm.

Amish Elvis sees the guy dancing and yells, "Stop the music!" Then he leveled a finger at the humiliated dancer saying, "Son, you don't dance to gospel music."

The crowd went ape.

The second time I saw Amish Elvis was not as pleasant. We had arrived early at an open stage event and had been among the first performers to sign up. I don't know how, but our names were erased, and Amish Elvis got our spot.

Now he was holding my capo hostage.

"Sir, could I have my capo back?"

"Son, you are a lazy musician."

"Excuse me?"

"Too lazy to learn the fretboard?"

"What are you talking about?"

"Don't sass me, son. I'm trying to teach you something."

Amish Elvis was in full Foghorn Leghorn mode, and it was drawing a crowd. Pickers old and young gathered around us. Amish Elvis read me the riot act about capos.

Apparently, he thought that using a capo was cheating, which explains why he called it a cheater earlier. He verbally let me have it for a little while. Then he dropped the capo in my hand and strutted off.

I stood there feeling lower than a snake's belly.

One of the old-timers I liked to jam with walked up to me and said. "Come on. There is something you need to see."

It took some coaxing, but I finally walked with him to a spot where we could see Amish Elvis on the stage.

"Aw, I don't want to see that fucker."

"Just wait. Be patient."

Amish Elvis introduced his first song. He tuned his guitar. He cleared his throat. He reached in his pocket and produced a large capo. Then he put it on his guitar and started to play.

My friend started to laugh.

"That dirty son of a bitch!" I growled as Amish Elvis sang and played with a cheater on his guitar.

A Show Of Shows

We marched in a loose formation through the concrete maze under the Philadelphia Civic center like gladiators decked out in satin and sequins. Our costumes glittered like disco balls. Some of us were burdened with massive backpieces fashioned from plywood and ostrich feathers. The feathers danced in rhythm as we marched. Banjos, saxophones, glockenspiels, drums, and other musical weapons of mummery were held tightly in our fists.

I was already starting to sweat under the heavy coating of clown white plastered on my face. My costume did not fit. The wide-brimmed hat they gave me to wear had a huge Styrofoam ax stuck on the crown. My heart was beating like a hammer.

As we marched past the other bands, somebody yelled, "Go get 'em, Overbrook!"

I was about to perform with The Greater Overbrook String Band. Like my father before me, I was now a Philadelphia Mummer – or at least I was about to be. Tonight would be a sort of trial by fire. I would be performing with the band on the opening night of the Philadelphia String Band Association Show Of Shows. I had only joined the band a few days earlier. I did not know the songs or choreography. I was riding along with the group like a leaf on the breeze, trying to figure things out as I went along.

To make matters worse, I was alone. Dad would be here for tomorrow's show, but he had to work tonight. I would have to face my inaugural performance without his support and guidance.

The group split in two, and we all began packing into a pair of large elevators. We were pressed in like a herd of beef dressed like Elton Johnn and carrying musical instruments. As the doors closed the oppressive push from all directions was almost enough to distract me from the fact that I was about to step out unprepared in front of a full house at the Philadelphia Civic Center.

The elevator rumbled to life. We all grumbled and jostled for position while other noises filled the air. I joked about being stuck in an elevator with a bunch of clowns gassed up on beer and hard-boiled eggs. Everybody laughed.

I had arrived not long before thanks to a ride from Tony Mantovani. I had to ride in the back seat for the whole trip because Tony kept his violin and bow on the passenger seat of his Lincoln Continental. Tony played Frank Sinatra and Dean Martin on the stereo. He had it cranked impossibly loud, but once I started to sing along as off-key as I could manage, Tony turned off the music.

We arrived at the Civic Center late. We had to rush down into the bowels of the building where we suddenly stepped into another world.

I had seen the Mummer's Parade before, but that is spread out over a day. We had just stepped into an area where all sixteen of the bands in the Philadelphia Mummers String Band Association were gearing up for the show. The air seemed to hiss from reflected light sparkling around us as sequins and rhinestones popped and flashed. Even with my hearing, the noise of so many conversations, groups rehearsing, feather rustling, instruments being tuned, and stuff being moved around was just overwhelming.

It was *wonderful*.

Each of the bands had an area marked off for the members to get changed. The Quaker City String Band had a tiki bar. Polish American String Band had this huge grill cooking kielbasa. Greater Overbrook had old guys from The Italian-American Club lavishing chafing dishes of meatballs with care.

The Italian-American Club was home base for the Greater Overbrook String Band. The building and the neighborhood it stood in existed in a bubble — a time capsule. The streets were clean. People were friendly. The barbershop at the end of the block gave terrible haircuts, but you could smoke, read Playboy, and listen to the regulars solve the problems of the world in the unnatural glow of marble patterned Formica. The club itself was surrounded by a walled courtyard. Inside there were bocce courts, a banquet hall, a nice restaurant, and a bar.

Since our last name is Costello, the guys at the Italian-American Club assumed we were Italian. My dad told me not to correct them.

"You're late!" One of the men barked at Tony. He pointed his meatball spoon in my direction. "Is that him?"

Tony nodded. A couple of guys pounced on me and started pulling at my clothes. I shook them off and put up my fists. There was a lot said in Italian that was probably insulting.

After a lot of hand gestures and gesticulations, somebody yelled, "You gotta get in costume! Come on!"

Oh.

As a crowd watched and laughed, I was stuffed into an itchy costume. An ostrich feather went up my nose, so I had a sneezing fit while they smeared clown makeup on my face.

I tried to snag a meatball and got my hand slapped. "After the show!"

With an ill-fitting costume on my body, badly applied makeup on my face, and an out of tune banjo strapped to my chest, I was now shoved into the lineup with the rest of the band.

The elevator doors opened to darkness. As my eyes adjusted to the light, I could see that we were backstage. There was a vast stage curtain in front of us. Everybody got into position as one of the talking heads from Philadelphia's NBC affiliate chattered to the crowd.

Rough hands pushed me to a position in the back of the formation.

The announcer's voice boomed over the sound system. The murmur of the crowd shook the air like faraway thunder. I was disoriented. I was asking myself why I get into weird situations like this. I wished my dad were there.

The banjo player to my right gave me an encouraging smile. "You'll be okay, kid. Just hold on to your banjo and try not to look stupid." He paused and gave me a good once-over before shaking his head and saying, "Just hold your banjo."

The announcer roared, "Ladies and gentlemen, The Greater Overbrook String Band!"

The curtain opened. The band started playing, and we marched out onto the floor of the Civic Center.

A string band performance is a musical medley built around a theme. The band plays while going through complex marching formations and choreography.

They put the strong musicians in the front line to keep things looking good. The lazy, clumsy, and inexperienced were placed in the back row.

I was in the back row.

As we stepped out to perform, I looked around in wonder. It was the most massive crowd I had ever seen. So many faces that they all became a sort of shifting blur. The roar of applause washed over us while popping flashbulbs blinded us.

The band began its performance. I was lost. The band went left, and I went right. The band went right, and I was running to the left, hoping to catch up. My pants were falling down. My banjo headstock hit the Styrofoam ax on my hat and pushed the brim over my eyes.

My bandmates were cracking up. The audience laughed as I ran around in circles, pawing the air like a drunken Russian circus bear.

The band finally marched close enough for somebody to grab me and push my hat away from my eyes. I was now two rows up and all the way over from where I had been. I looked around in dumb amazement wondering, "How the fuck did that happen?"

The guy next to me shouted, "We're almost done. Just stay close to me!" I stuck to him like glue for the rest of the performance.

Eventually, the chaos came to an end. The band blasted out the final note, and we marched back up onto the stage. The crowd was cheering, and I could not help but smile at the way the sound of applause changed as the curtain closed.

We marched back into the twin elevators. One of the banjo players got everybody in our car singing *My Ding-A-Ling*.

Back at Greater Overbrook's staging area, the guys started piling into the dressing area to get out of their costumes.

Dressing area? Then why did the old dudes get me changed in front of everybody? I guess they were screwing with the new guy.

I finally got out of my costume. I was too frazzled to think about the makeup I was wearing. I ended up getting clown white all over my street clothes and in my hair.

I staggered out, braced myself for some ball-busting over my terrible performance and got in line for a meatball sandwich.

"This guy!" One of the banjo players was patting my shoulder. "This guy goes out in front of all those people knowing nothing! He's a Mummer now!"

The guys all agreed. I, like my father, was now a member of The Greater Overbrook String Band. In less than a year I would march in the New Year's Parade down Broad Street on national television.

The crew from the Italian American club got me a meatball sandwich and a Coke.

The sandwich was indescribably good.

I can't imagine how we all looked. A crew of guys of different ages and backgrounds chowing down on meatball sandwiches with white makeup plastered across their faces. We were telling dirty jokes, singing songs, and swapping embarrassing musical adventures.

"Say, Pat. What's the funniest thing that ever happened to you?"

"A bunch of Italians dressed me up like a clown, humiliated me in front of a large crowd and fed me meatballs."

The rest of the weekend would have us doing several more shows. It would be better with my dad marching beside me, but tonight I had passed the test.

I was pondering getting up for another sandwich when one of the old guys handed me a fresh plate. He patted my cheek and told me that I was doing good.

I thought to myself, "I could get used to this."

On the ride home, Tony Mantovani let me ride shotgun while our instruments rode in the back. I took that as the night's greatest accomplishment.

B♭

Tiny was at the front door of the bar unhappily chewing an unlit cigar. He almost smiled when he saw me, but his face quickly fell back into a frown. "It's all cocked up." He said morosely.

My father and I were stunned. We had never seen Tiny down about anything.

"They are putting on some sort of a show. Got the stage set up for some smug asshole." Tiny said, gesturing at the door with his thumb. "I don't know how or if the Jam is going to happen."

My father and I were at a meeting of The Full Circle Music Society, a small group of folk musicians who met for a jam once a month around Reading, Pennsylvania. As folk song groups go, this was a good one. Sometimes the jam sessions were phenomenal, and sometimes they were rougher than sandpaper. Either way, it was always fun. The idea that we would be watching a show instead of jamming seemed crazy. I started to suspect that Tiny was playing a joke on us.

We went into the bar, and Tiny led us past the place where we usually jammed into a small banquet hall. As Tiny said, there was a stage set up with microphones. A geeky looking guy in a Panama hat was tuning his guitar and making noises bad singers think professionals make into the microphone. "Mmmmmmm-ah! La-la-la-la! Brooooooooom! Ma! Ma! Ma! Mmmmmmm*wah*!"

I just stood there. Frozen in disbelief. "Where did they find this asshole?"

My dad was equally unimpressed.

As I write this, I am aware that the three of us sound like cranky, judgmental bastards - and I guess we were - but this guy on stage was just a mess.

We couldn't bear to sit and watch the cretin do his pre-performance routine. We couldn't jam because of the vocalizing and tuning noises being blasted over the sound system. Tiny cracked a joke about how this guy probably made the same noises whenever he played with himself. I laughed so hard that the three of us ended up waiting for the jam to start outside.

The show/jam started. We all filed into the hall and sat sulking as one of the group leaders explained that the jam was still happening, but we would be starting with a performance by an old friend.

Dad, Tiny, and I all exchanged angry looks.

The guy in the Panama hat got on stage and talked about how he was an aspiring songwriter before breaking into *When the Red, Red Robin*.

Tiny groaned. "He sure as hell didn't write this."

Given that the song was a hit in the '20s, I was inclined to agree.

Another one of the guys who ran The Full Circle Music Society must have seen the expression on our faces because he came around behind us and whispered that we just had to be patient. Something was coming. If anybody else had said that I would have blown him off, but this guy was different. He was a good fiddle player, and he seemed to have a lot of experience under his belt. If he said something was in the works, I would be willing to give him the benefit of the doubt.

The show trudged along. The three of us waited. Waited. Waited.

Then it happened.

The man in the Panama hat was into his fourth or fifth song when suddenly there was a wail or a siren blasting outside the fire exit of the hall. Then a door was violently kicked open. Even though it was late in the afternoon, the room filled with midsummer sunshine, blinding us all.

There was an inhuman wailing sound that morphed into *Scotland The Brave.* A bagpiper in full kilt marched from the sunlight into the room and marched back and forth in front of the stage.

The place went crazy. People were on their feet. Some ran for the exits while others stood frozen in horror as the piper ran through his song. The sounds were monstrous in the confines of the hall. People were crying, laughing, and doing a weird sort of thing between the two. I could hear the shouts and cries over the cacophonous drones as the piper weaved his dark magic.

The man in the Panama hat sat on stage mouth agape. He was twitching like a reebok being taken down by a lion.

It was beautiful.

My father and I sat there, enjoying the show. I turned to see Tiny's reaction and found the old man playing his guitar along with the bagpipes.

Tiny shouted something at me. I could not hear him, but I could read his lips. "B♭!" Tiny yelled. "He's playing in B♭!"

I grabbed my banjo, tuned up my fifth string, and used my finger as an improvised capo. I quickly realized that the bagpiper was playing Scotland The Brave, so I started playing along.

I leaned over to my dad and told him, "B♭!"

He nodded and quickly started playing along on his tenor banjo.

Then the four of us, bagpipes, guitar, five-string banjo, and tenor banjo, played through Scotland The Brave a bunch of times while everybody else in the room went apeshit. It was glorious.

The song finally wound down, and the bagpipes faded away.

The performance had been a setup. The fiddle player had payback to deliver on the man in the Panama hat. The show at the beginning of the jam was a carefully crafted ruse. Once everything calmed down, we all got a good laugh. All of us that is except for the man in the Panama hat. He tried to be all smiles, but the gag had apparently hit him hard. It seemed like his confidence was blown.

We finally gathered for a jam session. It was good. The man in the Panama hat tried to join us, but he was still out of sorts from the practical joke that had been played on him. My father and I sang *A Shanty In Old Shanty* Town with Tiny backing us on his National guitar.

Before my father and I hit the road for home, I took a moment to talk with Tiny. I was blown away that we were able to play with the bagpiper. I wanted to know what other instruments I could jam with.

Tiny looked at me like I was an idiot. "You can jam with any instrument. It's only music."

"But how did you know what key to play in?"

Tiny shrugged. "He was in B♭."

I started to ask another question, but Tiny cut me off. "You'll figure it out."

The man in the Panama hat interrupted us with a broad forced smile and batshit crazy eyes. "Wasn't that a surprise?"

Tiny and I exchanged a look.

"Yeah, sure. A surprise. Fucking bagpipes." Tiny looked at me to say something.

"Umm. . . Fucking bagpipes."

An uncomfortable pause fell over us like a shroud.

"We liked your show." I lied enthusiastically — no sense in kicking the guy when he was down.

Tiny shot me a look of disapproval.

Far as I know, the man in the Panama hat never recovered. I sometimes envision him wandering the backroads of America clutching a guitar, humming like a bagpipe drone and warning passers-by about bagpipes like Elijah from *Moby Dick*.

One the ride home I pondered the mystery of how we played along with such an exotic instrument. In the years that followed, I had more opportunities to jam with instruments that seemed strange to me. From bass saxophones to musical saws, each encounter helped me understand how music works. To see the beautiful logic that makes music work.

A year later, I was helping Paul, the beatnik, host a banjo seminar. The workshop was part of an evening adult education program in an old high school. As we walked into the classroom, we passed a group in various costumes heading into the assembly hall, presumably to rehearse for a play or production.

As Paul and I were teaching basic frailing a loud wail rose from down the hall, slowly filling the classroom with the terrible roar of bagpipe drones. Then we heard it. *Scotland The Brave*.

I watched Paul and our students rise into a panic. I gently put my hand on Paul's shoulder and said, "B♭."

Paul looked at me in astonishment.

I nodded to the class, then down the hall and then back to Paul. "B♭."

Then he got it. I tossed him my capo as he gathered the students together and then ran down the hall.

I wondered how often people ran towards bagpipe music.

As I sat in the classroom, I could faintly hear Paul interrupt the piper, and moments later the two of them were playing together.

After a while, Paul led the students back into the room. Everybody was amazed that Paul could play with the piper.

I let Paul have his moment. That is what friends do.

Over time I studied music theory. The language of music turned out to be simpler than I had ever imagined. I finally began to understand what Tiny meant when he said, "It's only music." With practice, I could play anything with anyone. The world of music was open to me.

Mountain Music

The drive up into the mountains of Pennsylvania was so fast and wild that I am not sure where we ended up. I have tried many times over the last thirty years to retrace the route on a map, but it seems that some roads can only be traveled once.

At first, I thought my only reason for being on the trip was riding shotgun so that my grandfather could ride in the back. Eddie drove his massive old Chrysler as fast as it could go. He relied on a complex setup of radar detectors to get around the police. A constant stream of chatter from his hot-rodded CB radio helped him avoid speed traps.

My grandfather was afraid of nothing. He was scared to ride in the passenger seat when Eddie was driving.

The trip took place late on a September Friday night. Eddie took his version of a shortcut to his cabin, so we were flying down pitch-black mountain roads.

Eddie was talking to his wife Mary, who was also safe in the back seat, while the CB radio buzzed, and my grandfather prayed the rosary. Bzzz. . . "Mary did you bring. . . " Bzzz . . . "I always bring. . . " bzzz. . . "Hail Mary. . ." Bzzz. . .

Eddie was my grandfather's nephew. I think Eddie was one of the few people other than myself or my folks who could handle being around my grandfather. Eddie was always taking my grandfather out on electrical jobs or a round of golf. Eddie worked the old man too hard. I had hoped my grandfather would quit working with Eddie after he broke his neck on a job. No such luck. As soon as the hospital sent grandpop home in a halo traction device he was out wiring houses with Eddie.

I did not understand why, but my grandfather was convinced that making music was a waste of time. Grandpop wanted me to be a mailman. Yecch!

We were on our way to a little cabin Eddie had built. His kids loved the place so much that one of his daughters had married and started a family nearby. Mary was excited to see her new granddaughter. I was not tagging along to save grandpop from the terrors of riding shotgun with Eddie. I had been asked to come with my banjo and guitar for reasons Eddie had not yet shared with me.

Eddie's cabin was a lot like Eddie in a good way. Eddie was an electrical Jack of all trades. He had been a television repairman back in the days when you could repair electronics. His workshop at home was filled with old vacuum tubes and cool stuff that buzzed and sparked. His entire cabin was brimming with amazing vintage television sets of futuristic designs from the 1950s and 60s. Eddie turned them all on with the volume off to various UHF stations that were still broadcasting at the time.

Mary was busy in the kitchen. Soon she was calling us all in for corn on the cob.

Eddie had a unique way of keeping butter on his corn. He slathered butter on a slice of bread and wrapped it around the corn. My grandfather got upset about this.

Eddie was a big guy. My grandfather would be less kind and say that he was fat. Really fat. Whenever grandpop got on Eddie about his weight, Eddie would just laugh. This just made the old man mad because he was honestly worried about Eddie's weight.

I stayed out of it. If Eddie wanted to eat bread with his corn in his cabin while I was his guest, it was not my place to say anything. As much as I loved my grandfather, he sometimes did not know when to mind his own business.

After our late-night snack, Eddie asked me to get my banjo. I came back with the instrument and Eddie was setting up this old radio microphone. He had this crazy looking hot-rodded CB radio setup that was so overpowered it was almost a pirate radio station. He talked to a bunch of his friends for a bit and then asked me to play a few tunes. For the next hour, we sang old songs, and I played a few requests. By the time it was over, I was half asleep. I went upstairs and slept on my great-grandmother's feather bed. Happy as a pig in poop.

The next morning Eddie woke me up. I did not know what time it was. He was all excited, saying there was something I just had to do. It was a tradition at the cabin. We go outside, and he has this tiny motorcycle. It looked too small for anybody to ride safely. It was basically two small wheels with an engine in the middle, and it looked dangerous to me. I could hardly ride my bike around town without getting into trouble. No way in hell was I going to ride this contraption. Eddie says, "Come on; take a ride."

Motorcycles are bad mojo in my family. My father crushed his knee on one when I was little. Ever since then, a motorcycle was number two on my "don't you dare" list. Number one was doing drugs. I didn't even tell my folks when a friend was giving me a ride home from school on his motorcycle, and I got knocked off the back of the bike right in the middle of West Chester Pike. No way in hell was I riding this thing!

Then Eddie said, "Don't be a pussy."

So, I was riding this tiny motorcycle up the dirt road to Eddie's cabin. I had to ride standing up and hunched over because the thing was too small to sit on. My grandfather must have heard the little engine rumbling because he came running out of the cabin, yelling and waving. I was trying to figure out what he was saying and realized it was, "you're going to break your neck" just before I hit a root, lost control of the bike, flew through the air and landed on my back in a puddle. Some of Eddie's neighbors had heard the old man yelling and came running to make sure I was okay. I was fine. Just sore with a bruised ego.

My grandfather and Eddie laughed until they cried. I went in to get cleaned up and pick the gravel out of my elbow. Eddie and my grandfather took turns riding the tiny motorcycle by the cabin windows, waving at me as they went by.

After breakfast, Eddie and grandpop invited me to play some golf with them. There was a nice nine-hole chip and putt course close to the cabin. I was a little nervous. I stink at golf. I have problems with depth perception that makes a lot of sports difficult for me. I was terrible at baseball. I was so bad that when it was my turn at bat in the championship game my grandfather shouted, "For crying out loud, don't put him up! He can't hit!"

In golf, I could not get a ball to fly true. When I hit a drive, it shoots off sideways to the left or the right instead of going straight.

I don't mean it goes straight and veers off. The ball goes sideways off the tee.

The first-time grandpop took me to a driving range, I hit the ball and beaned the guy next to us so hard that he yelled, "Ow! Ow! Ow!" and fell. I wanted to help the guy, but grandpop just pretended nothing happened and dragged me away.

Grandpop said that only a genius or a goddamn moron could hit a golf ball sideways, and I sure as hell wasn't a genius. The game of golf meant so much to my grandfather who had worked as a caddy at the legendary Marion Cricket Club and had carried the golf bags of some of the biggest names in golf that nobody remembered but him.

I tried to learn the game, but my grandfather was a terrible coach. His idea of mentoring was better defined as hectoring. He screamed at me until his voice got hoarse, but my drives still went sideways.

Mom was always telling me that grandpop was very old, and he would be gone someday, and I would miss him, so I should take any chance to go out with him, no matter how mean he was. With that bit of Catholic guilt from mom in my mind, I agreed to go golfing with Eddie and grandpop.

The golf course was tiny. Each hole was just a chip shot and a putt. Easy, right? The course was set up along a river, and my first chip shot went right into that river. Eddie and grandpop just stared at me in horror.

"How the fuck did he do that?" Eddie asked the old man.

My grandfather shook his head and said it probably had something to do with my dad being Irish.

Eddie had a bunch of golf balls in his jacket pockets. He was hoping to use them to play a joke on my grandfather. We instead used them to replace the seven balls I hit into the river.

My grandfather tried coaching me. He said, "The next ball that goes in the river, goes up your ass!"

"Won't you have to jump into the river to get it?"

The one ball that didn't go into the river veered off into the woods.

"Is he doing this on purpose? Can somebody be this bad at golf?" Eddie asked grandpop.

My grandfather did not have an answer for that. At the ninth hole, Eddie grabbed my ball before I could hit it and threw it into the river himself. He said it would save time.

When we got back to the cabin, Eddie and grandpop were still mad at me about my screwy golf swing. I tried to explain that to play that badly intentionally, I would have to be the greatest golfer alive—and we all knew that was not the case.

Eddie's daughter stopped by the cabin to drop off her infant daughter. Mary was excited to have some quality time with her youngest grandchild. I went upstairs and took a long nap on that fantastic feather bed. I got up for dinner, and the baby was fussing. Mary tried everything in her extensive bag of tricks, but the baby would not stop crying. Everybody was getting frazzled, so I offered to help. Mary gave me an incredulous look.

"Okay," I said. "When you need me, just ask."

A few hours later, Mary asked me what I could do to help. My mother is an expert in early childhood development. I am a folk singer. We both have our tricks for soothing a fussing infant. Mom has modern scientific methods, and I have methods that are older than the hills.

I got my banjo.

"Banjo?" Mary looked worried. "I don't think a loud banjo tune will be much help."

"Don't worry. I won't play anything loud."

I gently tuned my banjo and started to play an old Irish waltz called *Rosin the Beau*.

The baby stopped crying. Then she started to laugh. I finished the song and as soon as I stopped playing, the baby started crying.

"In for a penny, in for a pound," I said. I started playing again.

I sat with Mary and the baby, playing my banjo until the sun came up.

It was great because it gave me a chance to spend some time with Mary. I knew Eddie because he was always at the house picking up my grandfather. Mary was almost a stranger to me. After spending a long night on top of a mountain serenading a crying baby, Mary and I were friends.

As I put away my banjo, I realized that my grandfather had been in the kitchen listening to me play for I don't know how long. To my surprise, the old man patted me on the shoulder and said, "You did good."

I was on cloud nine.

I went upstairs and got some sleep in that old feather bed convinced I had completed the mission the Tao had planned when I got railroaded into this trip.

Boy was I wrong.

I got a few hours of sleep before Eddie dragged me out of bed. He said that we were going to his daughter's house, but her neighbor was cooking a special dinner for me.

"For me? Why?"

"He is a musician. We have been telling him all about you, and now you are going to his place for dinner."

"Why didn't you tell me about this back at home?"

"You wouldn't have come."

"You got me there."

I was on my way to a cookout. I was hoping that this was not one of those setups where people only invite a musician to a party for the free music. That had already happened to me a few times, and it always sucks. We got to Eddie's daughter's house, and she had already heard via CB radio about my all-night concert for her daughter. Everybody was nice despite the awkwardness that happens when you are related to people but don't really know them.

Eddie got excited and dragged my guitar case out of his trunk. "Wait until you see his guitar!" he said as he began to fumble with the latches of my case. My heart was in my throat. To this day my guitar is my prized possession. Nobody goes into my case but me. I put down my soda and prepared to race across the room, but a soft voice stopped Eddie before he got the case open.

"Eddie, you never-ever touch another man's guitar."

That's how I met Yanis. He was of average height and slim build with ropy muscles on his arms and a dark beard covering a surprising amount of his face. He had a calm and deep voice. His eyes were those of a man with a lot of stories. I liked him immensely right on the spot. We all filed from Eddie's daughter's house to Yanis' back yard, where everything had been set up for a feast.

We ate in a large gazebo that Yanis had built by hand. I wish I had the words to describe it. The structure was big and sturdy, but at the same time, open and informal. It was obviously the work of a skilled woodworker. We sat down to one of the best meals I have ever eaten. All the vegetables had come from Yanis' garden. He grilled steaks perfectly, and I got to eat fresh clams for the first time in my life.

All through the meal, Yanis and I were trying to get a feel for how musically experienced we were.

"Have you been playing long?"

"I pick a bit."

"Is there a story to the guitar in the heavy case?"

"Hell, every guitar has a story."

Back and forth all through the meal. It was obvious we were both having fun. Eddie finally yelled, "Enough! Just start playing, dammit!"

We broke out our instruments. I tuned up my guitar and banjo. Yanis tuned his guitar.

We had a back and forth over who was going to call the first song. He said I should go first because I was his guest. I said he should kick things off because it was his place. He finally called out a Hank Williams tune. The hours after that went by in a blink. I let him take the lead, switching between my banjo and my guitar depending on the song or the tempo.

Yanis was good. Real good. The kind of good that makes you wonder why he wasn't famous.

He said something along those lines about me.

One of my favorite things about music is the way it allows you to communicate. You jam with a person on a lazy early

Autumn night, and you get to know that person better than you could over a thousand conversations.

Yanis sang one of the songs he wrote, and I played a banjo tune I wrote about my mother's spinning wheel. It was one of the best musical conversations I have ever had. We sang into the early hours of the morning, and only then did I realize that my grandfather had been watching us the entire time in near silence.

My Grandfather was never silent. He always dominated the party telling loud stories and snarking at young people who, in his opinion, did not know how to have fun anymore. Not tonight. Tonight, my grandfather had been quiet the entire time Yanis and I had been making music.

"You alright. Grandpop?" I asked the old man.

"Yeah. This was good. You guys can make music like they used to."

High praise from my grandfather.

Eddie finally broke the news that we would be heading back to Philly in just a few hours. Yanis and I shook hands, and he made me promise to come back soon. A promise I have as yet been unable to keep - but that is probably for the best. That night was a diamond — a rare and precious jewel. I could have come back for a thousand back yard cookout jam sessions and never come close to recapturing what happened that night.

When we got home, grandpop stopped making fun of my dreams of making music for a living. He even had me bring my guitar to play for some of his friends.

I have been welcomed into many homes across America and Europe in the years since that jam session. I have been the guest of some wonderful hosts. I still dream about the bright stars in the Pennsylvania sky over Yanis' gazebo and playing my harmonica as I leaned against my grandfather's bony shoulder while he sang, *It's a Long, Long Trail A-Winding*. In a lifetime of music, this was one of the best nights ever.

Finding Elmore

When the weather got hot in Philadelphia, the subway stations stank worse than usual, and the police became even more aggressive. I had to take my search for music teachers provided by the Tao to new digs. Preferably someplace with air conditioning.

That meant hanging out in the music store with Lefty.

The store was dead during the day. The air conditioning did not work well, so it was unbearably hot and funky. We sat and made music together as the world rolled by the store window. We sometimes had musicians wander into the shop, but they never wanted much beyond a set of strings or reeds.

The interesting musicians came in to rent sound systems by the night. A lot of the smaller bands would lease PA equipment for their gigs rather than shell out the big bucks for equipment that would quickly go out of date.

I met the Irish band that gave me my first gig while the leader was renting a sound system from this shop. That had worked out pretty well, so I was hopeful that my path would cross with another musician or band while I was hanging out with Lefty.

I liked Lefty a lot. We sang and talked for long hours and formed an unlikely friendship. His banjo skills grew stronger, and he started working with me on the guitar.

A long stretch of time passed with nothing happening. The local police had taken to raiding the music store, and the cops enjoyed roughing me up when that happened. They would fish my cigarettes out of my pocket and ask me where I got them. I would say that I took them from bad kids and that I told those bad kids not to smoke. That would get me bounced off the wall a few times. The police always got upset when they found Lefty's gun. He had a permit, so it was kosher, but the gentle officers would bounce us around some more – and I always had a smart remark that made everything worse.

Most of the time, I would sit on a broken amp and try to play my beloved Dobro 33H guitar. Solid bronze and chrome plated with the strings going over a spun aluminum cone that made this acoustic guitar almost as loud as an electric. Some of the best country blues was played on guitars like this made by Dobro or National back in the '20s and '30s. My guitar was a gift from my father. It was too much guitar for me at first. I could hardly carry it, and the fourteen-fret neck was as thick as a Louisville Slugger.

As hard as this guitar was to play, it drew experienced musicians like a moth to a flame. Lefty told me more than once that me playing my Dobro close to the window brought in customers. On this particular day, I had given Lefty his banjo lesson. Now I was sitting on a broken guitar amp happily butchering a Mississippi John Hurt song while hunched over my guitar so that my front teeth were resting on the Dobro's upper bout.

I am nearly deaf. My eustachian tubes do not work. I had endless ear infections growing up, and over time the conductive mechanics of my inner ear failed. My parents helped me practice speaking clearly, and I taught myself how to read lips and body language. Most folks can't tell that I have problems hearing. When I started playing the guitar, I could not hear myself, but I accidentally discovered that I could use my teeth to hear the instrument through bone conduction.

So, there I was in a sleazy music shop playing my Dobro badly when out of the blue I hear, "What the *fuck*?"

I looked up, and a middle-aged man was gawking at me like I was a geek in a sideshow. He started laughing and turned to Lefty.

"Why is Pillsbury gnawing on a guitar?"

They both started laughing. He made fun of my Converse high tops. He made fun of my Miami Vice tee-shirt. He made fun of my guitar.

I started to get mad.

"What's your problem? Never heard somebody play the blues before?"

He didn't just laugh at that. He screamed. I thought he was going to go into hysterics. He opened the shop door, leaned out and hollered to somebody, "Get in here and take a look at Pillsbury. He says he can play the *blues*!"

The next thing I know these guys come marching in and all of them think I am the funniest thing they have ever seen. I knew that I had a lot to learn on the guitar, but this was serious ball-busting. I was being mocked, and it didn't feel good, so I mustered up my courage and said, "if you guys are so great, why don't you teach me something?"

The guy who had started the let's laugh at Patrick party looked at one the others. They had a silent conversation, with one pointing to his watch and signaling that they had some time. The laughing guy pulled up a stool and sat in front of me. He reached for my guitar, and while it was hard to trust him, I handed it over.

"Damn, this is a heavy guitar. Okay, Pillsbury, do you know any bass lines like Elmore James played?"

"Who's Elmore James?"

"Who's Elmore *James*! You want to play guitar, and you've never heard of *Elmore James*?"

The rest of the group voiced their disapproval.

"Well, Pillsbury, this is what I'm going to show you."

He took my guitar and made the bass strings ring out in a boogie-woogie rhythm. He started simple and driving and changed the pattern each time through until he had this amazing walking bass happening.

"I want to play like that!" I said.

He handed me my guitar and took an electric from one of the wall racks in the shop. Then he looked over at Lefty who threw him a cable without saying a word.

"All right, Pillsbury, show me an E an A and a B chord."

I made the E and A the way I had been shown by my friend on the subway platform.

"The one-finger A chord is cool, but today make your A this way."

He barred across the first four strings at the second fret with his index finger and then fretted the first string at the fifth fret with his pinky. It sounded sweet.

"Now drag that chord shape so that your index finger is on the fourth fret and your little finger is on the first string at the seventh fret. That gives you a B Major chord."

Once he was happy with my A and B chords, he moved on to the bass strings.

"Sixth string open, Pillsbury, and."

I cut him off. "Stop calling me Pillsbury!"

"Do you want to learn this or not?"

"Call me Pillsbury."

"Sixth string open. This pattern works with the open sixth string while we fret along the fifth string."

He plucked the sixth string of his guitar with his thumb and then the fifth string at the second fret. This repeated as a pattern. The pulse of the open sixth string against the fifth string at the second, fourth, fifth and fourth frets. I had heard this before. This was the primordial boogie bass that has been around since forever. Bah-Bump, Bah-Bump, Bah-Bump, Bah-Bump.

"That's the bass line for E. Now let's play the A bass."

"How do I do that?"

"Just play the same pattern on the fifth and fourth strings."

I looked at him in disbelief.

"Is it that simple?"

He laughed. "Music is simple, Pillsbury."

We played a song by playing the E bass line twice, the A bass twice, the E bass twice, a measure of the B chord, a measure of the A chord he had taught me and wrapped it all up with the E bass twice. His friends watched us the entire time except for the guy handling the rental of the sound system,. He was hauling everything outside with Lefty.

One of them rummaged through my guitar case and seemed surprised to find a small copy of the New Testament along with some notes from my dad. I told him that that was the stuff that reminds me not to mess around with drugs or booze. They seemed to approve.

I was on cloud nine. My head was spinning with the possibilities of the boogie bass. "Thank you so much. I hope I get the chance to play this with a band someday."

The guys looked at each other and nodded. A couple of them went outside and came back with instrument cases. Somebody pulled a bass off the rack and plugged it into one of the shop amps. Another guy cleared the junk off the drum kit on display and began tweaking things to his liking. I heard horn players honking. In a matter of moments, I was sitting in the middle of a rhythm and blues band.

The laughing guy poked me and said, "Pillsbury, we're going to start in E. When I nod, go to the next chord change. We'll be using the E, A, and B chords."

I couldn't think of anything to say other than, "Let's boogie."

Suddenly I was in a sea of music. I could feel the air moving from the drum kit and the bass vibrations pulsing under my feet. Then he started to sing.

> *I've got a gal, she lives up on the hill*
> *I've got a gal, she lives up on the hill*
> *She said she was gonna love me*
> *But I don't believe she will.*

The laughing guy nodded at the chord changes, but even at that early point in my musical experience, I could feel the chord changes coming. We played and sang *Shake Your Money Maker* and rocked that funky music store like something out of a movie.

It was one of the best moments of my life.

Then in what seemed like the blink of an eye, the band had places to be. I tried to convince the band to let me tag along, but they made it clear that they were going someplace where I would not be welcome.

I shook hands with the band. I hugged the laughing guy. I am ashamed to admit that I never thought to ask his name. He called me Pillsbury, and I addressed him as sir.

After they left, I was still sitting with my guitar playing boogie bass and the subway shuffle. Lefty was watching me with an odd expression on his face. "Patrick, man, uhm." He seemed to be struggling to find the words. "You know that this isn't normal, right? I mean, shit like this doesn't happen. Blues bands don't set up in music stores to help kids learn bass lines!"

He had said this before, back with the Irish band. I had tried to tell him about the Tao back then, but he did not understand. So, I just smiled and said. "It does to me," and went back to my bass runs.

Busted!

The whole bar was jumping. The place always went nuts when we sang about Bobby Sands.

> *England you're a monster.*
> *Don't think that you have won.*
> *We will never be defeated,*
> *While Ireland has such sons!*

I belted out the chorus along with the rest of the band. As we basked in applause and cheers, the guitar player poked me in the shoulder.

"Is that your da?"

I looked from our vantage point on the stage to where the guitar player was pointing out into the room. At first, the layout seemed like it always did. Smoke hung in a ropy blue veil just under the light fixtures. Close to us, in true Irish fashion, the women were dancing together. Past the dancers, the men were doing some serious drinking. Past them and. . . Wait. Was that? How in the hell? Oh, sweet merciful Jesus. It was my *dad*!

Dad locked eyes with me. He gave me the same grin he always gets whenever he catches wise to my bullshit. He gave me a little wave, pointed at me, and then firmly pointed to the seat next to him.

The guitar player patted me on the shoulder. "You are fucked now, boy."

With his thick brogue and my terrible hearing, it came out like, "*U'er fooked now boy.*" I burst out laughing.

I waved back at dad and pointed to where my watch would be if I wore a watch.

He got the message. I would face the proverbial music when the band took a break.

This gig with the Irish band had grown increasingly surreal. There was an underground scene in Upper Darby rife with IRA ne'er-do-wells, and I found myself part of it without understanding one iota of it.

In addition to navigating unfamiliar cultural and musical waters, I was also trying to keep my nocturnal activities secret from my parents. There was also the problem of school. Some nights got so crazy that I did not bother going home, just going straight to school and sleeping in class all day.

Earlier tonight, after climbing out the window and sneaking away from the house, I had the nagging suspicion that somebody was following me as I hiked to the bar. I did not pay too much attention because the person never got close — and it probably did not help that I was running on little more than enthusiasm, nicotine, and caffeine.

The band finished its first set. As we sang about the bloody bloody British, I watched my dad talk to the regulars at the bar. Annie the owner. Pat the bartender. The guy who molested my banjo. The conversations seemed to go well. By the time we were wrapping up the set with the girls singing Carrickfergus, Dad was watching us intently. I could not read his expression.

The song Carrickfergus is a hodgepodge folk song, compiled over the years from many sources, so the lyrics make no sense – but it is a lovely mess. We had two girls in the band, and they sang together beautifully. I played my harmonica, mainly playing harmony with the voices of the women and the tinwhistle.

I figured that my father being here meant my time with the band was over. I decided to make the most of it, throwing myself into the music and drinking in the details of the experience and the wonderful song.

> *But the sea is wide, and I can't cross over*
> *And neither have I lovely wings to fly.*
> *I wish I could find me a handsome boatman*
> *To ferry me over, my love and I.*

The band took a break. I walked through the bar as slow as possible. By now everybody in the place knew that the kid with the banjo's dad was here. Folks were getting a good laugh at my expense.

I sat down. Pat the bartender brought me a Coke, patted me on the shoulder and gave me a wink.

Dad tried to look mad, but his face broke out in a crooked grin.

I did not bother to hesitate or mount a defense. "Did you follow me here?"

He nodded. "It was a longer walk than I expected."

I started to explain/defend myself, but dad cut me off. "I have talked to everybody here. They all love you."

"The big guy over there played my banjo with his dick."

"Yeah. I know."

"How do we sound?"

"Not bad."

I looked over my shoulder. My bandmates were not even trying to pretend that they were not eavesdropping.

"They tell me you don't drink."

"I don't want that. I'm just here to play."

He looked at me. "The fucking *IRA*?"

I shrugged. "At least they're Catholic."

"I never told you about my Uncle Jim. He came to America banging on his wooden leg cursing the British. I'll tell you about him later."

"Really?"

Dad nodded. He looked around the place and thought for a moment before bringing a laminated card from his pocket and tossing it to me. "This is a calling card with time on it. Keep it in your wallet."

"I don't carry a wallet."

He shook his head. "Just put it in your pocket. Use it to call home if you get into trouble. Any time, day or night."

He got up to leave as I sat there, stunned. I struggled to think of something, anything, to say.

"Be careful," Dad said, "Your mother worries." Then he was out the door and on the long walk home.

Somebody in the band blurted out, "He let him stay!"

We finished the set. Annie made me something to eat, and a crowd of us gathered at the bar to talk about my dad. That led to reflections from everybody about dads in general. Over strong coffee and the best roast beef sandwich in Philadelphia, I had friends and strangers draw close – some fuzzily shitfaced and others stone sober – to make me aware how lucky I was to have a father willing to let me follow my dream.

I played it casual, but the events of the night had rocked me to my core.

Walking home in the inky blackness that covers the city in the predawn hours, I stopped and sat on my banjo case by the side of the road. My father had given me the green light. It was as if a great weight had been lifted from my shoulders.

I had two roads before me. I could wander down the road to school and hang out until the doors opened. The other route would take me home, where I could have breakfast with my family and maybe shower the bar funk off of my skin.

I got up, picked up my instrument, and started down the road home.

The House of the Rising Bouzouki

Charlie looked like a Picasso of Robert Crumb. The face was familiar, but the angles and dimensions were just half a bubble shy of plumb. To add to the surreality, Charlie did not say much. He just gazed at me quietly with eyes made comically huge through his thick eyeglasses. Since I relied so heavily on lip reading and body language to communicate, Charlie's intense silence was maddening.

I was spending a September weekend with my parents at the French Creek Dulcimer Retreat, a neat little gathering of folkies. We met in a run-down camping lodge at a Pennsylvania state park. The camping cabins were masses of decaying wood, stone masonry, and buzzing wasps nests. I am sure that the cots were rusty torture devices left over from the Spanish Inquisition. The dining hall was so straight out of a cheesy slasher movie that I always expected to walk in on Jason Vorhees and Freddy Kruger chopping vegetables in the kitchen.

As crazy as it sounds, the funky location just made the weekend better. Sweeter. During the day, there were workshops where we shared playing tips on various instruments and then broke up for long stretches where we studiously did nothing.

The thing about French Creek that amazed me was that people tried to be kind. They did not always succeed, but they did try. Everybody watched each other's kids, meals were shared affairs, and the implied but unspoken rule was, "if you see a need, help out."

We originally came here for my mom. She had been playing the mountain dulcimer for ages, and she was hoping to learn more. My father and I fell in love with the gentle vibe of the place. We were the only banjo players in the group, but that was cool. It was kind of awesome being a baby alligator swimming with ducklings.

This particular year, my father and I were hanging out under the shade tree by the dining hall. I was sprawled out on the grass sipping on honeysuckle flowers and playing tunes with my dad when this massive sedan slowly revealed itself in the heat haze over the gravel road.

The car approached with an almost unbelievable slowness before coming to a stop in the middle of a field. I found this confusing because the parking lot was clearly marked. A car door the size of a bank vault swung open, and this tiny guy climbed out of the vehicle. He looked around aimlessly for a bit, spotted us and began heading in our direction.

"Dad?"

Dad was eating a sandwich at the picnic table. "Yeah?"

"Why do they always head for us?"

"What do you mean us? They come for you."

"Why me?"

"You have that sign floating over your head. The one only crazy people can see."

"What does it say?"

He chewed for a bit. "I think it says, 'Please come play with me.'"

I cracked up. Dad started laughing and choking on his sandwich. We were still giggling when Charlie walked up.

We introduced ourselves. I am not sure how Charlie replied because I could not tune him in.

As I have said before, I am nearly deaf. I adapted to my hearing loss by learning to read lips and interpret body language. This kind of interpretive communication requires that I get a feel for both how and why a person says things. In a lot of ways, it is like tuning to a radio station. Every person has a sort of signal I can fine-tune until I can understand them. Maybe they use their hands or have an unusual way of phrasing words.

Charlie had no signal. I studied him like a library book and got nothing.

Charlie talked quietly with my dad for a bit. I could not make out what Charlie was saying.

I took in what I could. Charlie's clothes were just a little bit strange. The fashions were old, and the clothes themselves were worn. His shoes were mismatched and different styles. His car. . . There was something off about his car.

"No license plates."

I turned to my dad. He pointed at Charlie's car. "He's driving a car with no plates." He shook his head.

"How in the hell is he ditty-bopping around with no plates? Is that even possible?"

"It must be possible. The car is here in front of us."

Charlie started pulling instruments out of his mysterious vehicle's cavernous four-body trunk. All of them looked homemade.

Not handcrafted. Homemade. A quality violin is handcrafted while my uncle's weird whittling projects are homemade — it's that delicate balance between the sublime and the ridiculous.

Then I saw the cobra banjo.

It was made entirely from wood. Even the banjo head was wood and braced like the top of a guitar. The neck ended in a headstock carved into a monstrous cobra with glittering glass eyes and brass fangs. The cobra's hood was open, with two friction tuners on either side.

On numerous occasions over the years, I have had priceless instruments in my hands. Charlie's cobra banjo still stands out in my memory. The craftsmanship was breathtaking.

"I don't like this one," Charlie said as he placed the cobra banjo back in the trunk. "This is my best one." He brought out something that looked like the love child of a ukulele and a baked potato. He reached in his pocket and brought out a gigantic triangular-shaped flatpick fashioned from the wing of a model airplane.

He said it was a bouzouki, but I met bouzouki players with the Irish band. This was not a bouzouki. It had a long neck like a bouzouki and an oblongish body like a bouzouki, but everything else was just a little off. Even the neck joined the body at an unusual angle that brought to mind H.P. Lovecraft's ravings concerning the horrors of non-euclidean geometry.

The bouzouki appeared to have been fashioned from scrap wood. The body was a complicated mess of Bondo and popsicle sticks. It was as ugly as any musical instrument I have ever seen. It looked like a caveman had tried to make a musical instrument from scraps of flint and saber-toothed tiger dung.

Charlie strummed a few licks on his bouzouki. It sounded lovely.

I guess they don't have to look good to sound good.

Next thing we know, Charlie is at our picnic table happily jamming with us and sharing the lunch we had packed.

The rest of the day went by in a flash. We had to keep moving our jam session to a new shady spot as the day rolled on. The three of us got comfortable with each other's quirks and started making music like we had been at it for ages.

Charlie's approach to making music was wildly different from ours, but once we stopped trying to fight or overthink the situation, we came together harmoniously.

That night the dulcimer retreat had an open stage in the dining hall. We performed in front of this enormous fireplace while the audience sat on rough wooden benches. The doors and windows were open and the September evening chill danced through the room with the warmth of the hearth.

My father and I performed together as *The God Knows We Tried String Band*. We were a little rough, but everybody – us *and* the audience – had a good time.

The guy who followed us was a stranger to me. He shuffled in on bare feet with a bad case of pillow hair, then he mumbled something to the audience about being tired and bored of us all, but he was willing to play just one song for us. He did a shockingly bad cover of *St. James Infirmary Blues*. The crowd was polite.

There were some great performances, too. One gentleman did a fantastic rendition of *Grandma's Lye Soap* and had a massive back spasm that required a gang of us helping him back to his cabin.

Once we had taken care of the guy with the bad back, Charlie and I got together to play *The House of the Rising Sun*.

What happened next is complicated.

We started playing. I was playing my banjo and Charlie had his bouzouki. I laid down the rhythm and started singing while rolling through the chord progression. Charlie took his bouzouki and went completely bonkers.

As Charlie grew more intense in his playing, I found myself in a curious mental state. Up until that night, I had viewed music as a task. Fret this string at that fret and strum that chord with these notes at a specific time. Everything was mechanical, and I hated it. Hated it. Hated it.

My dream was for music to become a way for me to communicate. My hearing cut me off from people. There was so much I longed to learn and share. Rumi's words from the 13th century burned in my heart like a brand.

> *Birdsong brings relief to my longing*
> *I'm just as ecstatic as they are,*
> *but with nothing to say!*
> *Please universal soul, practice*
> *some song or something through me!*

Up until now that Universal soul – God or the Tao or something else – had only sung through me in small flashes. Moments when the words, melody, harmony, and everything seemed to align for one shining moment. This happened a lot when I was playing with my dad. Sometimes with the Mummers and other times late at night with the Irish band. These had been fleeting, beautiful seconds of shining perfection that left me hungry for more – but anything I did to try and create those perfect moments only ruined things. The harder I pushed, the harder the Tao pushed back.

Tonight I was not trying. I was playing *The House of the Rising Sun* with a friend – and because we were not trying/working/applying conscious effort, that unknown something in the creative mind that allows artists to create, communicate and educate through their chosen medium was free to take over.

After the first verse, Charlie and I were in a groove. Each of us playing off of the other. Each of us creating the music from scratch as we played.

My mind was blank. I never gave a thought to what my left or right hands were doing. I had practiced long enough for the practice to take over. I made chords as they were needed without thinking about how to form the chord shape or even its name. There was no thought. There was no effort. Even the song was unimportant. We were making music. Together.

It was like a dance. We read each other's cues and responded wordlessly.

It was comfortable, beautiful, and completely free.

The song ended. Charlie and I grinned at each other.

The audience? They went nuts. I didn't care about that. The exciting thing for me was seeing my mom and dad up and cheering for us. That was cool.

That night stands out in my memory for several reasons. My parents got to see that I was becoming a stronger musician, which was very nice, but it was also my first glimpse at a different way of making music.

I saw a lot of Charlie after that. We had shared something that night, and moments like that create a bond. We never made music that way again, but I was always happy to see him.

In the years since that night, I continued to search for whatever it was that happened when Charlie and I played

The House of the Rising Sun. I was close to an answer, but I needed more pieces of the puzzle before that Universal soul would even consider singing through me.

Later that night, my father told me that he had paid for Charley's registration to the French Creek Dulcimer Retreat. I will always love him for that.

Before we went to bed in our rusty cots, with torn up cardboard boxes protecting our sleeping bags from the springs, I crept out to stare at the night sky and ponder the lessons of the day. There was much to learn, but the next lessons would come in their own good time. Tonight we had made a friend, made some excellent music, and kicked a little bit of ass. We were on our way to somewhere, and that was good.

The Parade

"Hey, Dad? Do you remember the hunting trip where it got so cold that bark was exploding off the trees and rocks were splitting in two?"

Dad nodded.

"Do you think we will ever be that warm again?"

Dad laughed, which was unsettling because his face was practically glowing with clown white in the predawn darkness. His electric blue wig and sequined Keystone Kop helmet sparkled in the streetlight. As he laughed, the steam from his breath plumed in the air.

We were standing in the staging area, waiting to begin marching with The Greater Overbrook String Band in the Philadelphia Mummer's Parade. It was so early in the morning that it was technically night. The wind bellowed through the city streets, building up strength and dropping in temperature until it whipped against our bodies like a battering ram. It was cold. We were dressed like clowns.

Sweet Jumping Jesus it was cold. It was brutally cold. The chill stung the skin, and each breath was like inhaling ice.

The frigid conditions would have been bearable with a winter coat, but our costumes offered little protection from the elements. Even the light cotton gloves on our hands were fingerless to avoid interfering with our banjo playing. The only thing between our asses and the January wind was thermal underwear, satin, greasepaint, and a lot of sequins. It was like being left at the South Pole wearing nothing but board shorts and sunscreen.

The parade was only starting, and we had already been up for hours. The band met just moments into the new year to start getting ready. Our costumes and makeup were elaborate, so it took time to get prepared before getting on the bus that would take us to Broad Street.

My father and I were both wearing costumes that included massive feathered backpieces, so we were wearing leather harnesses under our outfits. We were also wearing clown wigs, clown collars, and huge clown shoes. These additions made the already uncomfortable getup an almost transcendentally mind-bending experience.

"Hey, dad?"

"Yeah?"

"How do we take a piss in this getup?"

"Oh, you'll find out."

"What the hell does that mean?"

My father chuckled suspiciously. There was something he wasn't telling me.

In the dim urine-yellow glow of a streetlight, I spotted a guy dressed up in a vintage clown outfit trying his best to fight his drunken lack of balance with the need to lean over enough so that he wouldn't barf on the big ruffled collar around his neck. His face and bald cap smeared with grimy makeup. He wore a tiny derby cocked to one side of his head. A traditional Mummer's three-tier umbrella was in one gloved hand and a bottle in the other. I have never seen or heard a human being retch so violently. The spasms seemed to go all the way down to the soles of his oversized shoes.

Upchuck the Clown glanced our way. Our eyes met. He straightened up, shot me a drunken grin, yelled, "Happy New Year!" and danced a bit of the Mummers Strut before going back to tossing his cookies.

The Mummers Strut is a dance where you bend over at the waist – kind of like the South Philly Stoop where you hunch over to keep the grease from your cheesesteak from dripping on your shirt. Once you are hunched over like a bozo eating a greasy sandwich, the next step is to hold your arms out and dance in a circular sort of shuffle.

The reason Mummers do the strut comes down to our backpieces. Under our costumes, Mummers wear a leather harness to support famous gigantic ostrich feather backpieces. You probably think that ostrich feathers don't weigh much, but these backpieces were made of heavy plywood with a metal plate that slid into the leather harness to attach the contraption to my back. The framework was enough to make the rig dig into my shoulders. The feathers catch the wind, making it difficult to stand upright in even a light breeze. Try to play a musical instrument, march, and dance on a windy day in this getup, and you end up doing the Mummer's Strut.

You traditionally dance The Mummers Stut to the tune *Oh, Dem Golden Slippers* – a minstrel tune written in 1879.

To try and warm everybody up, the captain of our band got Harry, who more or less led the banjo players, to get everybody warmed up with some music. We got into formation, and the band played *That Old Green River* as we marched in place to keep warm. After the saxophones played the melody, the banjos kept ringing while all of us sang.

> *I've been sailing down that old Green River on the good ship Rock and Rye.*
> *But I floated too far; I got stuck on a bar.*
> *I was out there alone wishing that I was home.*
> *The ship got wrecked with the captain and crew,*
> *And there was only one thing left to do,*
> *so I had to drink the old Green River dry to get back home to you.*

We ran through a few more songs. *Powder Your Face With Sunshine, Margie, When You're Smiling, We'll Meet Again* and *Disco Inferno*.

As the sun began to rise over the City of Brotherly Love, people started gathering to see us warm-up before we took our place in the parade lineup. We played *Oh, Dem Golden Slippers*. The crowd cheered and danced The Mummers Stut.

My father and I were in different positions in the marching order. Out in front, gliding like a walking parade float, kissing babies and shaking hands, was our captain.

The captain of a string band works as a frontman during shows and holds the band together in the long hours of rehearsals and performances throughout the year.

After the captain is the front line, Dad was up there with the stronger banjo players. Then are rows of horn players, the pit band, drummers and bass players. We had dancers too, but they were always shills paid to march - not part of the actual group. The guys who could march in full costume with a bass fiddle strapped across their bellies seemed inhumanly strong.

The very last row is pretty much for the clowns. Troublemakers. Wiseasses. The last row in our band usually filled with guys smoking, telling jokes, getting handed beers from the crowd and getting kisses from the pretty girls.

I was in the very last row, naturally.

It was great being in the back because we could do pretty much as we pleased.

We had been through several dress rehearsals for the parade. That prepared me for the difficulties we faced marching, dancing, playing instruments, and singing while wearing all of our gear. What caught me off-guard as we started to step out onto Broad Street was not being able to hear.

I could usually hear enough sound to pick up the rhythm of a song. I am also really good at feeling chord progressions, so most of the time, I can figure out a way to continue making music. This morning, out in the winter air with the roar of the crowd and the echo of our music bouncing off the tall buildings like a pea in a tin can I was utterly lost. I couldn't even hear myself complain about not being able to hear.

When my last bit of hearing was overwhelmed, I found myself faced with a choice. I could give up and ride out the parade in the warmth of the truck, or I could cowboy up and find a way to make do. After a couple of blocks, I acclimated to the environment enough to play and do the choreography. My hands were too cold to do anything complicated, so I kept things simple.

The air smelled of winter chill, exhaust fumes, urine and the press of hundreds of bodies along both sides of Broad Street. The city towered above, beyond, and around us. The air seemed alive with bits of feathers, confetti, glitter, and smoke raining down on us. My brain tried to take in the crowd, but it was just too big – a virtual sea of faces and waving arms.

We sang and played as we marched, stopping every few blocks to run through the production we would be performing for the judges at the end of the parade route. Things were moving slow, and word came down that one of the string bands was performing at every block.

Mummers never back down from a challenge. We all started performing at every block. The crowd loved it, but it tripled the workload for the band.

In addition to the extra work, I had to pee. How in the hell was I going to manage that in this costume?

After hours of marching and performing, we got to a spot on the parade route that was set up for the Mummers to take a pit stop.

We broke out of formation. I walked around to the front line to meet with dad.

Dad points to the right and says, "You can piss over there."

I look over, and there is this clumsy partition made of two-by-fours and black plastic. Mummers in full costume were going behind the barrier in a hurry, and strolling back out refreshed.

"Can I get out of my costume?"

Dad laughed. "Nope."

So, we go behind the wall. I was innocently expecting some sanitation like a urinal or even a bucket, but the Mummers were pissing on the ground.

I looked at dad.

Dad shrugged. "What were you expecting?"

So, standing awkwardly next to my father and the rest of The Greater Overbrook String Band I started trying to work out how I would relive myself while wearing all of my gear. Even finding the fly of my costume with my chilled fingers seemed like an impossible task.

 I will spare you the details, but I eventually managed to get myself in position when I looked down and realized I had to try and piss over my clown shoes. I couldn't spread my legs because the wind would catch my backpiece. I couldn't lean over, lean back, or see where I was aiming. I tried standing on one foot.

A cop was watching me disinterestedly. As if a banjo playing clown covered in sequins balancing on one foot pissing on Broad Street in broad daylight was perfectly normal. I wiggled my raised clown shoe clad foot at him coquettishly and in a singsong voice shouted, "Happy New Year!"

The cop rolled his eyes and left. The guys around me cracked up.

My father was watching me with a mixture of amusement and dismay. "You look like a dog looking for a place to shit."

A guy dressed like Liberache's vision of an Inuk picked a spot next to me. Then a bunch of guys dressed in vintage Mardi Gras outfits. All of them struggled with their costumes, instruments, and backpieces.

I managed to pee without falling over. Given my costume and outfit, this accomplishment probably qualifies me for NASA.

I stepped out from behind the partition and noticed that all the urine was running down the street. Gallon after gallon of swill rolling down Broad Street and into the crowd. It was like being at the racetrack with my sketchy cousins.

All I could think was, "God, I love Philadelphia!"

A cup of hot coffee and a sandwich later, we were whistled back into formation to begin marching again.

The rest of the parade went by in a blink. I could write an endless string of adjectives without coming close to describing the experience.

As the sun set down over the city, we were still marching. It was almost dark by the time we performed for the last time and were finally able to take off our backpieces and climb up into the welcome warmth of the bus.

I started to take off my banjo, but dad stopped me. "We're not done yet."

I was so tired I wanted to cry, but I was sure my tear ducts were frozen solid.

The bus whisked us through the dark city back to Overbrook where The Italian American Club was putting out a spread for us – we just had one more job to do.

Out of nowhere, Meatball yells, "Wait. . . Where is my dad? Did you bastards do it *again*?"

Everybody on the bus started to laugh.

Meatball was one of our drummers. He was a nice kid. Always came to practice. Never complained. One of the guys.

Meatball's dad was not technically a band member, but he worked all year making props, helping out and doing all kinds of things to help keep the band running. He was such a good guy that it would be going against Mummer tradition not to screw with him, so every year the group found a way to distract him long enough for the bus to take off without him.

It was mean, childish, juvenile, and funny as hell.

Meatball looked around the bus trying to be mad, but he ended up laughing with the rest of us.

We got back to the club, and you could smell the food cooking out into the street. We go in, and the place was empty. We all filed into a small room at the back of the bar and found ourselves on the set of a cheesy gangster movie.

The lights were low. Seated at a table, back to the corner, was an older man in expensive-looking clothes. He had a camel hair coat draped over his shoulders. His hair was perfectly coiffed. The lenses of his glasses had a rose tint. His fingers were weighed down with rings. His watch was too big and too obnoxious to be a knockoff. He was drinking wine and smoking cigarillos.

Behind the man in the fancy suit stood two hulking guys in dark suits wearing light-colored ties. They were wearing sunglasses inside in a dark room. They were standing very still.

Our captain approached the well-dressed man. The slick-looking dude slipped a slug of cash to the captain as they shook hands. Then he patted the captain on the cheek.

What the hell was this? The Italian mobster stereotypes were getting piled on so thick and heavy that I was sure this had to be a joke. I couldn't help but chuckle and ask the guy next to me what was up with the gangsters.

"Shut up, Patrick," was the tersely hissed reply.

I shot him a questioning look.

"Where do you think you are? Who do you think pays for these costumes? Shut up. Be respectful. That is the real thing."

Oh shit.

Then a lot of the unusual things I had noticed about Overbrook like the lack of crime in the neighborhood started to make sense.

The captain asked the man in the fancy clothes what he wanted to hear. He said, "*Margie*. I love that one."

We started to play. The horns took the melody and then it was up to the banjos to strum while the whole band sang.

> *Margie, I'm always thinkin' of you, Margie*
> *I'll tell the world I love you*
> *Don't forget your promise to me*
> *I have bought a home and ring and everything*
> *For Margie, you are my inspiration*
> *Days are never blue*
> *After all is said and done*
> *You are still the only one*
> *Oh, Margie, Margie, it's you*

As tired, cold, and hungry and sore as all of us were, the song sounded fantastic. The Boss clapped and sang along while his bodyguards glared at us from behind their sunglasses.

When the song was over, The Boss got up and shook all of our hands. He started to pinch my cheeks but stopped short when he realized that he would get clown makeup on his immaculate hands.

Then we all piled into the banquet hall and stepped to Italy.

The Italian American Club had put superhuman effort into a meal for the band. The old guys must have been cooking all day.

Have you ever seen *Goodfellas* or *A Night At The Opera*? Remember the Italian food in those movies? This was like those cinematic experiences only a million times better. Fresh bread, pasta of every description, and more and more and more.

It took the band time to peel off our costumes and get back into street clothes. None of us bothered to take off the clown makeup because our families and the men who had prepared our meal were all waiting patiently for us. Not one person was served before us.

I looked around as my bandmates stuffed their faces. By now, all our makeup was smeared, so we looked ridiculous.

Meatball's dad managed to get a cab to the club. He wanted to kick all our asses, but then the guys got him so drunk he loved us all again. It got a little weird when he started rubbing my head saying, "I like this foul-mouthed little creep," over and over again.

I was so tired it was hard to keep my eyes open before ingesting a fuckton of carbohydrates. Now I was half-punchy — time to go back home.

We talked all the way home, each of us recounting events of the day in the green glow of the pickup truck's dashboard light.

We were both hurting from head to foot. Bodies chilled to the bone with fingertips still numb from the cold air and twelve hours of constant playing.

We walked up to our front door. Dad paused and smiled at me.

"Good job."

"You, too!"

"Tomorrow work begins for next year's parade."

"Let's worry about that tomorrow."

We headed inside, footsore, and painted up. Mom and grandpop rushed to hear all about our adventures.

That is when I realized there is one thing in this world better than marching in the Philadelphia Mummer's Parade with your dad: coming home.

The Great Jam-Buster Beatdown

"*Quiet*! You'll wake up mother!"

Big Jim delivered the filthy punchline with his deep voice, and my father and I collapsed helplessly into laughter.

Big Jim played a garbage can bass. If you made the mistake of calling it a trash can bass or a washtub bass, you ran the severe risk of being on the receiving end of a classic Pennsylvania Dutch tongue-lashing.

The bass itself was fashioned from an old galvanized garbage can secured upside-down to a slab of plywood. A short length of clothesline attached to the galvanized soundboard served as the instrument's single string. A broom handle served as the neck of the bass. Jim changed the pitch of the notes by pulling back or leaning forward on the broom handle. The instrument was slathered in a seasick brown paint job. An antique milk can with a cushion glued to the lid served as a stool.

It should have sounded pretty bad. Most washtub basses sound to me as if some crazy person fed beans to beluga whales. Jim's garbage can bass was unique in that it actually sounded pretty good.

Jim himself looked like the movie *Witness* had been crossed with *The Road Warrior*. A big Lancaster County Pennsylvania Dutchman, Jim had the Amish-style Shenandoah beard. He was tall with ropy muscles and a potbelly that stretched his suspenders.

Jamming with Jim was always a treat. His bass playing was surprisingly creative, and it was fun swapping jokes and road stories with him between songs.

I was with Jim and my dad at a little festival. We got there early to find a shady spot, and that was a smart thing to do because it turned out that this field only had one or two small shade trees. Everything else was just out in the open under the summer sun.

We set up our cooler under one of the smaller shade trees and started making music. I was playing banjo and guitar, dad on tenor banjo and Jim on his garbage can bass. The three of us were having a grand time, and we welcomed anybody who wandered along, looking to join in.

A bluegrass band started loitering on the outskirts of our session. We motioned for them to join us, but they remained strangely stoic. You could tell they were in a band because they all pretty much dressed the same. You could tell they were into bluegrass because they were not having any fun.

All around us the field was still mostly empty. There were plenty of places to jam without intruding on anybody.

After lurking for a while, the band formed a tight circle about three feet from us and started beating on their instruments like they caught them breaking into their houses.

We were being jam-busted — lucky us.

Jambusting is a bluegrass trick where a band goes into performance mode to drown out every other musician within range. It is a childishly cruel and ugly trick stemming from a genre that has struck me over the years as seemingly hell-bent on generating childishly cruel and ugly behavior.

We had a shade tree.

The bluegrass band had decided that we did not deserve said shade tree, even after we tried to make them welcome.

The bluegrass band tried to play loud enough to drown us out and drive us away.

The band was giving it everything they had, hitting the strings hard enough to throw their instruments out of tune.

I exchanged looks with Jim and my dad. From what I could read from his lips, Jim was weaving an elaborate tapestry of profanity while my father just looked pissed.

The trouble with bluegrass is that it is not a genre as much as it is a brand. To fit in, you have to sound, look, behave, and think like every other bluegrass fan or run the risk of being ostracized. We were different, and in the bluegrass playbook that meant we should be drowned out, humiliated and have our shady spot taken over by brigands.

They did *Molly and Tenbrooks*, *Shuckin' The Corn* and *Hot Corn Cold Corn*. It wasn't bad. They were competent. In a more normal situation, we could have made music together. Alas, the band was determined to bully the three of us.

Unfortunately for them, the bluegrass guys did not know who they were fucking with.

I thought to myself, "So it's a fight they want. Okay, Dobro time" and put my banjo down. I picked up my massive bell-bronze Dobro 33H guitar and started putting on my fingerpicks. I nodded to dad. Dad nodded back.

The bluegrass band had just tried to bust the wrong jam.

I grabbed an E chord on the guitar and started mixing the shuffle pattern I had learned on the subway with the boogie bass from the blues guys in the music store. Dad began to chop out a rhythm, and the two of us went into *Sweet Home Chicago*.

I was singing at the top of my voice. I was playing my guitar hard enough to overdrive the resonator cone. The instrument set out rippling wave after wave of bass and treble in whatever direction I was facing.

I pointed my Dobro right at those jam-busting philistines.

Our instruments seemed to come alive. I was singing and shouting with gravel and spit in my voice.

For a fair distance all around us, jams were stopping, and people were looking around, searching for the source of the music.

Right next to us, the jam-busters were starting to look confused and worried. They were beginning to realize that they were trying to bully the wrong musicians.

I will give them credit; the bluegrass guys tried like hell to hold themselves together. For a few moments, they were able to muster up enough grit to set their jaws and dug in their heels, but we were overpowering them, overwhelming them.

They tried to play *Foggy Mountain Breakdown*. We sang *Troubled In Mind*.

It was like that terrible Charlton Heston movie where army ants overrun a coffee plantation, only transformed into a musical where bluegrass snobs discover that this thing called the blues not only exists but it is stronger and wilder than anything they imagined.

We switched back to *Sweet Home Chicago*. The rippling rhythm of my guitar and the chop of the banjo made it hard for them to stay in rhythm. The volume of our playing made it hard for the band to hear each other. The little pause we threw into the chorus to make the titular line stand out completely threw the bluegrass guys out of rhythm.

Eventually, Jim joined in on the garbage can bass. His big hands were slapping the clothesline, sending deep bass vibrations into the ground beneath our feet.

That was the final blow. The bluegrass band scurried off like rats from a sinking ship.

"Yeah! Take that! Fuckers!" Big Jim growled as he gave his garbage can bass a good slap.

As the band stalked away, they brought to mind images of hyenas glowering and chattering after getting their asses beat by a pack of lions.

"If the shoe fits," I thought to myself, "wear it."

Our music had carried far and wide over the festival grounds. Pickers came running to join us. Pretty soon we had a nice crowd sharing the cool shade making just about every kind of music on God's green earth.

As the rest of the day went along, we had a few other bluegrass groups come around to bust our jam session. After a few dismissed attempts at inviting the reprobates to join us, we just had some fun and played so loud and with such distracting rhythms that they all ended up leaving us in peace.

We have run into jam busters many times over the years, and the phenomenon still puzzles me. Heck, bullies, in general, intrigue me. I cannot fathom what drives a man to take a beautiful thing like music and twist it into a way to push people around.

I wish the bluegrass pickers had joined us that day. The powerful thing about music is its universal nature. People talk about genres, comparing this music to that music – but every song in Western civilization was created using the same twelve notes. You do not need to limit yourself or specialize in just one kind of music. You do not need to try and bust up a jam just because those other musicians look different or prefer a different sound. A good musician can play with anybody and learn from everyone without losing his or her unique voice.

If you do find yourself confronted with jam busters, don't get upset. Be nice, be welcoming, and be hospitable.

Never let them see just how well you play at first. Speak softly and carry a honking huge Dobro 33H.

Tennessee Flat-Top Barf

Take me back to the place where I first saw the light
To the sweet sunny South take me home
Where the mockingbird sings me to sleep every night
Oh, why was I tempted to roam?

Ted played and sang beautifully, and his tenor voice sailed out in the hot summer air. I was learning the beautifully bittersweet melody as we jammed. Some unknown stranger was listening to us intently. We were smoking, our cigarettes tucked into the headstocks of our guitars, sending out plumes of smoke that we hoped would scare away some of the mosquitos and biting flies.

The biting insects seemed to appreciate the nicotine rush because the biting increased.

The stranger pushed his grimy baseball cap back on his head. "You boys need to pick faster. Pick us up a breeze and scare these bugs away!"

. . .Okay.

I was having a hard time playing my guitar because this weird spotted hound was trying to insert himself between me and my instrument. I assumed the dog belonged to Ted or the nameless stranger.

We were sitting on the front steps of our new home in Crisfield, Maryland.

Crisfield is a geographic anomaly or wormhole in that it takes a three-hour drive to begin any trip out of the area.

You may think I am exaggerating, but it is true — three hours of driving through flat terrain. No hills to break up the skyline. Nothing but pine trees, chicken farms, and salt marsh for one hundred and eighty minutes before you can start driving from point A to point B. There are folk tales of tourists going mad from these flat roads. Friends who visit me compare it to driving on the moon.

We found Crisfield by accident many years before. As we drove through the small town on the banks of the Chesapeake Bay, my father despaired, "Who would want to live in this godforsaken place?"

It turned out that we were exactly the kind of people who wanted to live in this godforsaken place, after all. A few years after our initial visit, we wound up buying a home in Crisfield.

Crisfield was a sleepy town that seemed stuck in the 1950s. Our new home was a funky old place with wide front steps going up to a screen porch that was perfect for jamming.

I started playing on the front steps every evening almost as soon as I moved in. They rolled up the streets around 8:00 PM back then, so the road was always quiet after dark. Perfect for sitting with a banjo or guitar and singing to the stars.

After a few nights, my neighbors started coming out on their porches and opening living room windows to listen to me play.

A few weeks later Ted showed up as I was sitting down to pick a few tunes. He had a guitar with him, so I said, "Let's pick!"

Ted was a portly gentleman from Culpepper, Virginia. He had a summer home near the end of our street.

Every time I looked at Ted, I got this weird sense of *déjà vu*. His face was shockingly familiar, but I could not draw anything up from my memory banks.

I let Ted take the lead. He started singing and strumming his guitar. I backed him up and sang some of the choruses with him. The whole time I am wondering, who is this guy? Is he a famous picker? Was he on the news?

Jamming with Ted that night I learned some of my all-time favorite songs. *The Sweet Sunny South*, *Two Litte Boys*, *I'll Be With You In Apple Blossom Time* and *I'll See You In My Dreams*.

As we were playing, a ratty pickup truck started doing slow drive-bys with this wild-looking driver hanging out of the window trying to hear us. It got annoying, so I waved to him and motioned for him to join us.

His name was Melvin. He worked at the county dump, but right now he was on suspension for dressing up a bunch of porta-potties as voting booths. He had a guitar at home, but right now he just wanted to listen to Ted and me make music.

A scroungy blue-tick hound fell asleep on my lap. It was all skin and bones. Weak as a kitten. I figured it had to belong to either Melvin or Ted.

Ted and I started singing again, and it was going fantastic. The music was flowing, an old dog was asleep on my lap, and the neighbors were all clapping and making requests. I smiled at Ted, and the memory came back to me like a bolt of lightning.

"Hey, Ted. Have you ever been to the Gettysburg Bluegrass Festival?"

"Oh, lots of times. I try to go every year."

My eyes narrowed. "Do you own a poncho?"

Melvin puffed on a discount brand cigarette that smelled like burning fingernails and secret regrets. "I don't know what's going on, but this just got exciting!"

I repeated my question. "Do you own a poncho?"

Ted frowned. "that's a weird question. If it will shut you up, then, yes. I do own a poncho."

"Ever barf all over a banjo player's shoes at a campfire jam?"

Ted's eyes grew wide. "That was you?"

"You! You barfed on me!"

"Call 911!" Melvin yelled, "There's gonna be a fight! Holy shit! I came for the music, and I got a soap opera too. Whoo!"

I liked Melvin immediately and immensely. I couldn't help but laugh. "There's not going to be a fight. We are just caught up in the middle of a poetic coincidence."

Melvin gave me a pleading look. "I have got to know. After what just happened, you have to tell me!"

Ted hung his head. "Tell him."

So, I told Melvin the story.

It was my first bluegrass festival. My father surprised me with tickets, and then the stripper-preacher wound up tagging along.

My father and I had started as bluegrass banjo players, but the techniques and the culture surrounding the music drove us to search for the sort of freedom we eventually found with frailing banjo. Now that we were starting to become more skillful, we wanted to explore the possibility of playing old-time banjo in a bluegrass setting.

I spent several weeks before the festival taking care of my two young cousins on a Christmas tree farm. The experience had been quite a test. I nearly killed myself more than once learning to drive the tractor. The first time I tried to burn the trash as instructed, I started the fire with gasoline by mistake and accidentally created a garbage mortar that burned off my eyebrows, sent flaming diapers into the afternoon sky so high that one must still be in orbit and left the two children in my charge dancing and shouting, "Do it again! Do it again!"

My cousin Barbra appreciated me keeping an eye on her sons, but I think she may still be angry with me over what happened to her dishwasher.

After playing Mary Poppins for a while, getting to the bluegrass festival was a treat. I was so excited to get out and start picking.

The first musician I met was a friendly young man who was playing a brand new Gibson Earl Scruggs model banjo. He went on to explain that he bought the expensive instrument and then went on to replace almost everything he could with costly custom parts to make it sound better.

It still sounded like a banjo to me. I decided to treat the situation the same way I did when people talked to themselves on the subway: be pleasant, but keep my trap shut.

As the sun went down, the stripper-preacher and I went out looking for a jam.

I had played in a lot of bars by this time in my life, but even I was shocked at the amount of drinking going on.

The festivals and jam sessions I had attended before this had been friendly and open affairs where every kind of person, instrument, and music was as welcome as the flowers in May.

In bluegrass, things were wildly different. The jams were closed circles. Anybody trying to kick back and listen to the music was forced to stare at the backs of the musicians.

In the folk scene, the goal was to get everybody participating at some level. We all have music in us, and we all need a place to come together to make music for the joy of it.

Bluegrass seemed to be about recreating specific performances. Even a jam session was treated like a stage show. Creativity was implied as something inferior to slavishly replicating every note from an old record. The stress and pressure seemed to be insane.

As we wandered from camp to camp at Gettysburg, I had a sinking feeling that I did not belong here.

We finally came across a jam that did not seem to be in a tight circle. We stepped up to the fire, introduced ourselves, and asked if we could join in.

"Wrong banjo." The voice came flatly from just outside the campfire glow. "Open backs don't belong in bluegrass."

What the hell is this? The opening of *2001: A Space Odyssey* only with less hirsute primates?

I shook my head and sighed in disgust. "It's just a fucking banjo. Can I join you or not?"

Somebody else spoke up. "Sure. Let's pick."

The songs were unfamiliar to me, but the rhythm and structure were repetitive from song to song, so it didn't take me long to fall into step with the group.

These guys could drink. I had been around drunks and stoners before, but this crew took things to a professional level. As they got drunk, the circle tightened until we were eventually almost shoulder to shoulder around the campfire.

The fire was too hot. The music was getting a little stale. Alcohol was fuzzing up the rhythm of the pickers in different ways, making it harder and harder to stay in time as the jam fell apart.

I was standing between a skinny mandolin player and a portly guitar player wearing a poncho.

The ponchoed guitarist was singing *Lamp Lighting Time In The Valley* when all of a sudden he turned in my direction with his face painted by shadows and flame as it contorted in a violent spasm of nausea. He leaned over his guitar. His jaws worked violently open as he gagged before vomiting all over my shoes. I stood frozen in horror watching my feet get hosed down with voided beer, liquor, unnamable globules and globs of gristle.

The life of a banjo player takes you to extreme places. I have been chased out of a church by sword-wielding Lutherans in the heart of Dresden. My cousin Eddie and I once destroyed the governor of New Jersey's office with a highly pressurized jet of stale rice and beans. I have had food poisoning in the bathroom stall of a Trailways bus going down a stretch of highway so full of potholes that the bus would go airborne like NASA's Vomit Comet, leaving me – and whatever had just come out of me - floating for a moment in zero gravity. So believe me when I say I have been on the receiving end of some things that would scare the buzzards off a gut wagon – but this guitar guy barfing on me took the cake.

I stood there transfixed, frozen to the ground like a deer in the headlights.

Poncho straightened back up, wiped his mouth with the back of his hand, and said "That's bluegrass" before going back into *Lamp Lighting Time In The Valley* as if this was normal.

The stripper preacher staggered off, trying not to throw up.

The group jammed on as if nothing had happened. I tried to get some kind of reaction, apology, joke, or even an insult, but they were pretending nothing happened.

I washed my shoes best I could at a water spigot and walked back to camp barefoot.

Dad laughed himself to sleep when he heard the story.

As I told the tale, Melvin clapped like a child. "This is just Fan-*tastic*! I got music, a fight and now a story! A tale of tales!" He turned to Ted, "How does it feel to have your new neighbor turn out to be on the receiving end of a drunken booze-spew? I mean, what are the odds? We should go buy lottery tickets?"

Ted tried to change the subject, asking me if anything good had happened at the festival.

I sighed. "Pete Wernick gave a banjo workshop that could have passed for a time-share sales pitch and answered all of my questions by telling me to buy his book. So I went to talk to Ralph Stanley. Ralph was trying to sell his banjo to a yuppie, so he told me to get the fuck away from him. Then

Ralph sent Curly Ray Cline to apologize and give me free stuff, but I didn't take any of it. I liked Curly, but not Ralph. To hell with that old bastard. "

Ted and Melvin gaped at me in opened-mouthed horror. Even Melvin was unable to come up with any commentary on that one.

I finished my thought. "No, Ted. Nothing good happened outside of a weekend with my dad. You wrecking my shoes was the high point of the weekend."

The dog was still sleeping on my lap as I sang some more songs with Ted. We sang about home and mother and God and country. We sang about hookers and beer and gamblers and murders. Ted sang the modern American bawdy ballad *The Scotsman*, so I upped the ante with a few verses of what could be one of the filthiest songs ever written: *The Ball of Ballynoor*.

I don't know what the neighbors thought when I got Melvin and Ted to sing the chorus with me.

> *Singing "Bow to your partner,*
> *with your ass against the wall,*
> *If you cannot get laid on a Saturday night,*
> *You'll never get laid at all!"*

Ted talked about meeting old medicine show performers when he was little.

I told some stories from my time with the Irish band.

Melvin had a few good stories too.

We sat late into the night, smoking, picking, swapping stories, and singing. By the time we realized that it was time to head in for the night, we were friends. In spite of the barfing on my shoes thing or my lack of appreciation for Ralph Stanley.

Ted walked down the street to his home. Melvin lingered a while longer, not wanting the night to end.

Eventually, Melvin got into his pickup truck.

The dog was still on my lap.

"Hey! Don't forget your dog!"

Melvin laughed. "That's not my dog. That's *your* dog."

"I don't have a dog!"

He laughed and shouted, "You do now!" before driving away.

The dog and I headed inside. It was a male blue-tick coon hound that looked like the last five miles of rough road to death's door.

I took the dog inside. I picked up the phone and called my dad. "Pop? Remember the guy that barfed on me at Gettysburg? He's our neighbor now! I just jammed with him!" I paused for a second. "We also have a dog now. His name is Queequeg."

By the next morning, Melvin and my neighbors all knew the story. The family from Philadelphia was okay. Friendly, excellent musicians and to top it off, the boy has a blue tick hound!"

At long last, the Costellos had a hometown.

Hootenanny!

The walls were shaking. The floor vibrated with the tapping of dozens of toes. The big display window rattled with the energy of so many people singing and hands clapping in rhythm. Mothers held babies by their arms so that the children could dance on the tables. We sang *Bad, Bad Leroy Brown* and *The House of the Rising Sun*. We shouted out *Wreck of the Old 97* and *That Good Old Mountain Dew*. *Big Iron*, *Freight Train*, *Wildwood Flower,* and *Careless Love*. *The Baltimore Fire* and *The Saint James Infirmary Blues*.

A more motley band of minstrels never had so many people singing along as us. It was one of the most powerful and positive musical experiences of our lives – and by the time it was over, we would lose what I thought was a lifelong friend.

It all happened at a hootenanny.

What's a hootenanny, you ask?

Well, a hootenanny is an informal gathering of musicians with an emphasis on group singing and audience participation. During concerts, lectures, and performances the audience is expected to shut up and sit quietly. At a hootenanny the audience is expected to raise hell. When we got word that a hoot was taking place in Coatesville, PA, our reaction was excited disbelief. The hootenanny is a rare beast in this day and age. Dad called the venue to verify, and we were assured that this shindig was indeed going to be a hoot – and, more importantly, we were welcome to come and play! I reached out to our old pal

Paul the beatnik and we agreed to meet there. We made the three-hour trip seem short by singing and laughing all the way from Crisfield, MD to the venue.

We got to the coffee house, and the place was really nice. We would be jamming in the lobby of a freshly restored theater. We walked in, and my heart sank. A crew of self-proclaimed experts in old-time banjo was setting up a sound system on the right side of the huge lobby. These were the banjo snobs who had thrown temper tantrums when my father and I began posting free banjo lessons on our web page in the late '90s. They did not look happy to see us. I plastered a grin on my face and introduced myself to the guys setting up the microphones. I was met with sneers and cold looks.

Shit, I thought to myself. We drove all this way, and now we would not get a chance to play. My father and I grabbed a table on the left side of the hall, got a cup of coffee and decided to jam a bit before the show started.

As we were quietly playing a few songs, a guitar player who had also gotten the cold shoulder from the banjo nerds asked if he could join us.

The more the merrier!

The guitar guy felt really out of place with his long hair and Iron Maiden T-shirt. We didn't care about that because music is a universal language. The guitar guy was not used to playing an acoustic guitar. He played an electric axe in a rock band. To make him comfortable we played *The House of the Rising Sun.* He rocked out, and with every sweet note his body twitched violently. As we moved on to *Saint*

*James Infirmary Blue*s a bass player who has also gotten the cold shoulder from the banjo geeks asked if he could join us.

The more the merrier!

Now we were a quartet.

While we were playing the coffee house started to fill up. A large crowd gathered around our table. Another guitar player joined us after getting the silent treatment from the dastardly banjo bastards. We were now a quintet. Iron Maiden Guy on lead guitar, Epic Beard Man on bass, Meticulously Dressed Guy on rhythm guitar, Dear Old dad on tenor banjo and Yours Truly on the five-string banjo. We could not possibly have been more different individuals, but we came together like peanut butter and jelly. More importantly, we connected with the crowd that had gathered around us.

I try to avoid getting into confrontations, so I was a bit worried about our jam interfering with whatever hellish experiment the banjo squad was cooking up. Then the owner of the venue approached and thanked us for making music. Our jam kept going, and the crowd grew larger with more and more people singing along and making requests.

Paul finally arrived, and I rushed to embrace my old friend. He hit me up for parking meter change and then asked me to feed the meter for him.

Yeah, nice to see you too.

I came back in, and Paul was with the banjo crew. As he talked to one rude bastard another made faces and jagoff motions behind his back. It was ugly. I tried to tell Paul that we had saved a space for him at our jam, but he wanted to stay with the haters. I went back to our table, feeling confused.

By now the lobby was divided in half. On the right, there was a group of banjo nerds sitting on stools talking about banjo into microphones. The only audience on the right side was Paul. On the left, our quintet was surrounded by a mob of people. The crowd shouted out requests, and we either played the song or faked it. We were having a ball, and everybody in the room was loving the music. Paul came over. I started to make room for my old friend.

"Patrick, you guys have to stop! They are doing something important over there, and you are ruining it!"

I gawked at him in disbelief.

"Paul, they advertised a hootenanny."

"You always get hung up on definitions. Don't you ever want to fit in?"

"If I wanted to fit in, I never would have taken up the banjo."

Paul left. Angry.

Our hootenanny continued.

The banjo dimwits turned up the sound system. Horrible feedback filled the room. Everybody laughed and went on singing. *The House of the Rising* Sun got played again. The banjo brigade started their show. From what I could gather, each banjo dude was talking about a fiddle tune called *Old Molly Hare* and then playing it a few times before the next guy would take over and talk about *Old Molly Hare*.

As this was happening our improvised Quintet was playing up a storm. *The Story of Bonnie And Clyde*, *The Green-Green Grass of Home*, *Me and Julio Down By the School Yard* and on and on.

I saw Paul complain to the owner. The owner nodded and started walking through the crowd to our table. "Oh shit, this is the end of our fun," I thought to myself.

"Hey, guys. . . could you play Bad, *Bad Leroy Brown*?"

Dear Old Dad hollered back, "of course!"

We kicked off the song, and then the magic happened. I wish I had the words to properly describe the experience, but something this Zen has to be lived to be understood. Words can't do it justice. The five of us came together and played the song a million times better than we ever could alone. The crowd felt it too. People danced, and people sang. People got a little weird. It was a perfect musical moment. Then Paul started banging on our table, yelling for us to stop.

When the song was over, I gave Dear Old Dad the signal that it was time for us to go.

As we packed up our gear, the five of us shook hands and exchanged phone numbers. The crowd – and the owner – were sad to see us calling it quits, but the banjo boobs were having a tantrum. I guess that they did not know a hootenanny is supposed to be a group singing event.

I went over to talk to Paul. He was distant at first, and when I thought he was going to talk to me, all he did was ask about the parking meter. Dad came over to say hello, and Paul turned his back to us and walked away. My father and I stood in mute disbelief.

We never saw Paul again after that. I ran into him online a few times, but our relationship had changed.

A few days after the hootenanny word got out about what had happened. Some versions of the tale painted my father and me as musical bullies. Others claimed that our improvised quintet was a professional band. They always left out that the gathering was advertised as a hootenanny - or that we had the blessing of the venue's owner.

A year later, the meticulously dressed guitar player made to trip to Crisfield to visit us. We talked about the things folk musicians and guitar players like to gossip about, and we broke out our instruments for a jam on our front porch. He brought up the hootenanny and the phenomenon that occurred while we had been playing Bad-Bad Leroy Brown. "I have been trying to make it happen again," he said.

I shook my head. "That was a one-time thing. We could play that song a million times without seeing anything close to it. We were just the right kind of tired and distracted. The room had this crazy energy fueled by the crowd".

My dad added. "You can't repeat stuff like that. Chasing it will get you nowhere. You live it and then move on. Play over and over until it happens again."

"Dad," I said. "That was pretty Zen for an Irish Catholic."

Our guest stayed a little longer, but the visit really ended when he realized that we had no secret formula to share.

Paul passed away about a year later. I sat at my computer and wept for my long-lost. . . I don't know what to call him. He was never my teacher, and the way he blew us off after the hoot made me wonder if he had been a friend. I guess it doesn't matter. We loved him, and we always made a place at our table and our jam sessions for him. He chose to walk away wearing a turd for a breastplate.

I almost forgot! The event went on for a short time, but they changed the name from "hootenanny" to "old-time banjo demonstration." I can't say how it went because we never went back. We went on to attend other festivals and sometimes even host events of our own, but those are other stories for another time.

I still think back to that moment at the hootenanny when everything went Zen as we sang *Bad-Bad Leroy Brown*. We still watch parents with children whenever we play in public. If a mom or dad has a baby dancing along with the music, we know that we are on to something good.

It's A Sin

When we started billing ourselves *as The God Knows We Tried String Band*, people in Crisfield, Maryland, assumed that we were a gospel act.

Locals would say, "They have to play gospel music. They got God in the name of the band, don't they?" and then go on to invite us to perform at a potluck supper or some such thing expecting us to play songs like *Rock Of Ages* or *The Old Rugged Cross* in a church hall full of Methodists eating tuna casserole.

The problem was that we didn't know that much gospel music. When you grow up in an Irish Catholic household, Protestant hymns are not something you hear all that often. Our idea of gospel music was stuff like *I Saw The Light* or almost bluegrass tempo versions of *Uncloudy Day, When The Roll Is Called Up Yonder* and *Will The Circle Be Unbroken*. The Methodists didn't know how to handle that much rhythm in their music, and more than one performance was interrupted by somebody getting up and witnessing.

The first time that happened I didn't quite know what to do. Dear old Dad and I were just sort of standing up there with our guitars and banjos wondering if we were supposed to leave or start playing some rousing background music like *The Battle Hymn of the Republic* to add some drama. It kind of upset the rest of the folks too because they already knew the stuff the penitent was witnessing about. Crisfield is the kind of town where everybody knows each other's business, so the guy who was pouring out his heart and unburdening his soul wasn't really dishing out any news that hadn't already been discussed weeks ago over coffee at Gordon's Confectionary.

Sometimes the witnessing was kind of surreal. There was this one service that featured a preacher in a red wool suit (it was the hottest day of the year, and the hall had no air conditioning) talking about *Barabbas*, but he kept calling him *Barnabus*.

"And they said, give us Bar-knee-bus!"

Pop said that he was just trying to show everybody what the hell was going to be like if we didn't all behave. I allowed as I was going to be good from that point on.

After a while, the folks started inviting us to play our music rather than hymns. I felt kind of weird the first time we tried playing *The Old Rugged Cross* only to have somebody in the back row yell out, "Play *You Dirty Old Egg Sucking Dog*!" I glanced over to the preacher who nodded and said something about God having a sense of humor and to just go ahead and (sigh) play the song about dogs that (an even deeper sigh) suck eggs.

We just became part of the church scenery throughout the town. Given that there are more than twenty churches in Crisfield that was an awful lot of pot-luck suppers. To this day I can't see Jell-O without breaking out into *In The Garden*.

We were two Catholic folk musicians who didn't quite get the whole Protestant thing but were part of the family anyway. Every once in a while, we would crank out our overdriven version of *I Saw The Light*, but after Miss Gladys the head church lady got up and hollered, "I can't listen to this. I'm not Church of God; I'm a Methodist!" as she ran out of the room, we figured it would be best if we stuck to playing Folk and Honky-Tonk Country in the church halls.

We were invited one weekend to play with a traveling preacher from Tennessee and while I was kind of hesitant after my past experiences with folks witnessing, I figured, "what the heck?" and agreed to be part of the entertainment at the revival.

The traveling preacher was this little guy with a big white beard who had this sort of vibe going with him that is hard to describe. He really believed he was doing what he was put here to do, and he honestly loved God. He preached like he was introducing people to his best friend. I know that might sound kind of hokey, but this guy was just cool.

The revival wasn't as much of a culture shock as I thought it would be. The evangelist knew how to preach in a way that wasn't too big on the fire and brimstone stuff, and he was a pretty good guitar player. By the time he was getting ready to move on to the next town, I liked and respected the guy. He didn't even blink when people asked us to play *You Dirty Old Egg Sucking Dog*. He just played along with us and pointed out afterward that God even loves egg-sucking dogs.

Right before he was getting ready to leave, he complimented me on my guitar playing, and I did what I almost always did back then. I went into to whole, "Aw, shucks, I'm not really that good" routine.

The next thing I knew the preacher turned on me just about as angry as I've ever seen anybody. He was jumping up and down and waving his guitar like he wanted to bonk me over the head. I was trying to figure out what I did or said to upset him while Dad was looking at me from across the room with that, "What have you gone and done now?" look when the preacher started talking.

"I gave you a *compliment*. I was trying to tell you how much I enjoyed playing the guitar with you and your dad and you turn around and insult me. How could you?"

I started trying to say something, but he was in full-blown Southern preacher mode. He wasn't talking angrily anymore; it was worse than that. He was talking passionately like he really wanted me to understand this.

"False modesty isn't just a sin, Patrick. It's *insulting*. When somebody gives you a compliment about your music that person is trying to say, 'Hey, thank you for sharing with me!' and when you start that sandbagging routine you're telling that person that he's stupid, and even worse you're trying to get them to keep stroking your ego telling you how good you are. When a person comes over to compliment you, they might want to ask you about something else, like as an icebreaker, to lead into maybe asking for help learning the guitar. If you love music so much, why would you want to drive that person away? Is it so hard just to accept the compliment like a man and say, Thank you?"

It was one of the few times in my life that I didn't have a snappy comeback. I just stood there and waited for him to catch his breath. After glowering at me for a moment, he said, "You play very well, Patrick. I really enjoyed your music."

I grinned at him. "Why thank you, Pastor Charlie."

He shook my hand and said that there was hope for me yet.

Ever since then, I have tried to avoid making the common guitar player's mistake of answering a compliment with the "aw shucks" routine. The amazing thing about it is that the preacher was right. Nine times out of ten, the compliment is an icebreaker. My honest and direct, "thank you" is usually the opening for the person to say how he'd always wanted to play the guitar or the banjo and I always wind up sitting down and going over the basics with him or her. I make a new friend, and I get to do what I love to do by sharing the licks and tricks I picked up from the cool old dudes with a new musician.

It's easy to do the false modesty thing. Sometimes it's hard to accept compliments because people are, by nature, pretty bashful. Looking somebody in the eye and just saying thank you takes, as the preacher pointed out, a measure of character.

So, when somebody tells you that you have done a good job, even when you are convinced otherwise, just smile and say, "Thank you." You'll probably make a new friend.

And if you ever hear *You Dirty Old Egg Sucking* Dog being played at a tent revival, I guess Dear Old Dad and I are to blame.

Just This Banjo

We came back to Chester County and Old Fiddler's Picnic. It was foolish to try and go home again, but there is something about a hometown that calls from the past. I wanted to see what had changed while longing for everything to remain the same.

It is more than a four-hour drive from Crisfield, Maryland to Coatesville, Pennsylvania. With a person with diabetes driving and a person with epilepsy in the passenger seat, this is a hellish drive. This was further complicated by the fact that Crisfield is geographically situated to be three hours from everything. To make the trip more manageable, we arrived the night before and stayed at the Holiday Inn Express across from the Exton Mall.

When you live in Crisfield, the Exton Holiday Inn Express is downright swanky.

We arrived the next day at Hibernia Park. We intentionally arrived before the event so that I could have some time alone in this special place.

Tiny was long gone. I saw him one last time a few years before we left Philadelphia. He was worried about me throwing my life away to make music.

"Music isn't a job, kid. There's no money in it. Don't you know that all of your heroes died broke, drunk and crazy? There ain't no happy endings in country music!"

I tried to reassure Tiny that I would be okay. I did not care about money or show business. I just wanted to make music. There was more I wanted to say, but you never know when you will be seeing your friend for the last time. I saw no sign of him the rest of that season or the next or ever again.

While my dad happily set up our jamming area in a shady corner of the woods, I leaned into the breeze and whispered a greeting to Tiny and my other long lost friends and mentors.

After a while, I jammed with my dad and watched the crowd slowly filter into the field. Old-timers with instrument cases stepped through the rough pasture with exaggerated care. A light mist hung gently over the grass like a veil. Birds sang from the trees lining the festival grounds. The early sunlight painted everything with color. The scent of fresh-cut grass hung sweetly in the air.

My grandfather always said that Pennsylvania was the most beautiful state in the Union – which is complete bullshit if you have ever seen even a blurry picture of Maryland, but that is beside the point. On a morning like this, I could agree with him.

"I love this place," I said to my dad.

Attendance at the festival was down by a huge percentage since our last visit. The crowd of musicians and spectators that once filled the forty-acre field had been winnowed down to a corner of the park. It hurt to see the changes, but change is part of life. Better to focus on the joy of the moment and celebrate. Here. Now. Today.

My father and I sang all the songs we had learned over the years since our inaugural visit here. At first, it was just the two of us, but over time a crowd began to gather. People were bringing guitars, banjos, fiddles and all manner of other instruments to jam with us. We had to sing at the top of our voices to get past the roar of strumming guitars and mandolins.

Old friends began to show up. I couldn't believe it when our old bluegrass banjo teacher – the chain-smoker with an epic mustache – was playing along with us. More familiar faces and then. . . Grandpop?

It felt unreal to see him here. My grandfather was dying. He had been exposed to Asbestos working at the Navy Yard during both world wars, and the fibers had done their evil work.

As sick as he was, my grandfather was not going to miss Old Fiddler's Picnic. He somehow convinced one of my uncles to drag his wheelchair to the park.

The old man was happily clapping to the music and hollering at the top of his lungs with joy. Between songs, he reached out to anybody within grasp, pointed at me and said, "Did you hear that? Did you hear him play? I'm Al Groff, and that's my grandson!"

There was no time to get choked up. Whenever we finished a song people crowded in on us with questions. Kids wanted to know about my Dobro 33H. An old man wanted help tuning, and a soccer mom asked how to make an E chord.

I thought I heard Tiny laugh, but it might have been my dad.

I stuck a cigarette in the corner of my mouth, draped my arms over my guitar and said to the crowd, "All right. Show me what you've got."

It would have been perfect if the day ended at that moment, but it got better.

Later, I wheeled my grandfather aside so that we could talk. There were things I needed to say.

I told my grandfather that I loved him. I apologized for not being a better grandson. That I knew he wanted me to learn a trade, but music was what I needed.

He looked at me and said, "I'm proud of you. I've always been proud of you."

The words should have come with a roll of thunder to shake the ground. Proud of me? Him? How? Why? I had never heard him say anything remotely like this in my life. My throat clenched up, and tears started welling in my eyes.

Then it hit me. The same sort of calmness that I feel when I am making music. He put to words a truth that I had always known.

"I know that, PopPop. I always have."

He nodded silently.

We spoke until there was nothing left to say. There was nothing left to do. We sat together on that little hill at the edge of the field — he in that cursed wheelchair and I on the green Chester County grass. On the stage, a fiddler kicked off a fair rendition of *Faded Love*. I leaned over and rested my head on his arm as the music played.

We went back to the jam session. I broke out the banjo, and we played *The White House Blues* for Tiny. The jam rolled on and on. With my grandfather's blessing cool and soothing like a balm on my brow, with my father – my best friend – by my side, we sang the songs of yesterday and celebrated in the moment. There was nothing between us and the uncertain future — just this banjo.

Copyright Notice

As I was finishing up this book, the launching of impeachment hearings against President Trump was the breaking news headline. Every channel seemed to have angry people yelling at other angry people.

Seeking a reprieve, I went online and found more of the same anger everywhere I looked. A directionless cloud of rage that was eerily reminiscent of the Day of the Dove episode of *Star Trek*.

My father and I always advise our students, "if you see a need, fill it." So, in defiance of the negative emotions of the day, I am making Just This Banjo freely available online.

Maybe, just maybe, the encouragement, support, and love I experienced will come through the pages and inspire even one person to stop being angry.

I was the least likely music student to ever fret a string. I was able to learn my craft because there were kind and decent people in the world – and that has not changed. Hopefully, my adventures will inspire you to, as Woody Guthrie put it, "*vaccinate yourself right into the big streams and blood of the people.*"

If you like the book, the eBook edition will be available for purchase at http://frailingbanjo.com.

You may also consider sponsoring our work on Patreon: https://www.patreon.com/Dobro33H

If for, some reason you can't stand the book, donate to charity in the name of somebody you don't like.

Patrick Costello
Crisfield, Maryland
Autumn, 2019

Made in the USA
Columbia, SC
20 May 2020